The Truth Of Your Reality
333 A Conversation Between Myself And The Universe.
By
Wade Stephens.

Contents

Introduction. 3
Chapter 1 7
A Little About Me. 7
Chapter 2 29
The Mind Trap. 29
Chapter 3 58
Releasing Ego And Fear. Discovering The 'True Self'. ... 58
Chapter 4 76
Separating The Creator From Religion, And Walking Forward. ... 76
Chapter 5 97
The Pine Cone. 97
Chapter 6 105
The Mark Of The Creator, ... 105
Intelligent Design. 105
Chapter 7 117
Everything Is Connected And Everything Is One. 117
Chapter 8 133
Be The Change. 133
Chapter 9 137
Connecting With The Universal Consciousness. 137
Chapter 10 142
The 33 And 333 Phenomenon. 142
Chapter 11 162
The Final Chapter 162
The Revelation. 162

Introduction.

This is a book from the heart; a journey that I now understand began from the moment I was born. I am now at the point of my journey where I feel I want to share with as many people as possible what I have discovered.

I can show 3 truths and a call for action from all, that have been revealed to me by what can only be described as a higher force, or God. Not the biblical God that has been created in the image of man. Not the angry God that needs pleasing with endless prayer and endless sacrifices, but rather a loving, harmonious, conscious energy that connects all and what brought about the very existence of our Universe as we know it.

I have rewritten this book so many times and tried not to use the term God, mainly because a lot of people will naturally shut down the instant this term is used, but when it comes to light that we live in a conscious Universe and that there seems so much evidence that point toward a creator, then I truly find it difficult to use any other term than God. I will naturally give evidence later in the book regarding these bold statements.

Some of us are taught by our peers growing up that you cannot believe in God and believe in science simultaneously and yet I seem to have found tons of scientific evidence that can prove clearly a creator or underlying force exists, compared to not finding anything scientific at all that could explain the atheist belief. The only answer that would cover the atheist belief is spontaneous creation, and any logical scientist knows that spontaneous creation does not happen, ever.

Any atheists that wants to throw into the discussion the 'Something from nothing' scientific theory then I ask you to read the scientific papers regarding this subject. Our understanding of the vacuum of space being nothing is a wrong understanding. It seems the vacuum of space is full of potential energy and so not really worthy of the title 'nothing'. So, we will shut down that argument right now. Below is an excerpt from Scientific American.

1. *'A vacuum might seem like empty space, but scientists have discovered a new way to seemingly get something from that nothingness, such as light.... One bizarre consequence of this uncertainty is that a vacuum is never completely empty, but instead buzzes with so-called 'virtual-particles', that constantly wink into and out of existence'.*

Atheists often use science has a point of argument, and yet the people that actually understand the field of science and the world around them the most often have the strongest belief in God.

Let us start smack bang in the centre of everything, and look outwardly from ourselves. What is reality? Is there a reality that displays an underlying truth for everyone?

For example, a worshipping Muslim will live and die with the reality that God exists and will in his or her own lifetime fulfil certain practises to ensure an afterlife in heaven. This is the Muslim's reality, it is true to that perspective and when this person dies naturally their own reality and the Universe in which the individual lives dies with them.

Now consider the atheist, the nonbeliever that lives and dies with the belief that God doesn't exist and that when they die they simply die. This again is the reality to the nonbeliever and when he or she dies so too will their reality die with them. Both live within their own reality, but in the same Universe and with both examples their unique belief is only true based on their own unique view to 'what is'. So, what is reality?

Reality it seems is that what we choose to create and believe. So, it appears that there is no fixed reality. Like God created the Universe, we are able to create our own reality within it. And this reality (the one you live in) exists simultaneously alongside billions of other realities. Everything combining to form what is a shared reality that functions as a whole where we live under the laws imposed by society. Like God in miniature we seem to be able through our own actions to create our own reality.

Does this not open endless possibilities to the adventure and reality we exist within? It certainly shows us that it truly is our own unique view of things that constructs our own unique reality.

With this outlook toward reality and our ability to choose our own Universe in which we exist, the purpose of this book is to deliver a message that is eternal and a message sent for each and every one of us. A message of truth, a message of understanding and a message of divine importance.

What this book discusses has been spoken before; it is only now though, in this modern age and with new advances in science that I can bring forward evidence of an underlying force of creation to the Universe. This is what I bring in this book; evidence scientifically that gives you the reader the opportunity to perhaps see things that you have never been shown, and to make up your own mind regarding the truth of your existence.

This has been a journey my whole life, and as crazy as this sounds I never realised the intention of this book until I reached the final chapter, even though I have been writing it over a few years. It seems the Universe or God does this a lot with us, at the time we don't fully understand why we are in a certain place at a certain time but inevitably at some point the dots join and it all makes sense.

A few years ago, I began having a strange relationship with the numbers 333 and 33. Waking at 3:33 and seeing 33 or 333 everywhere, it seemed something was slowly getting my attention. I only mention this briefly now as it was these signs that led me on this path of 'discovery, learning and understanding'. Naturally this will be elaborated on later in the book.

This journey has given me a connection and a closeness with our creator through my own particular journey, and it is one I wish I could describe. Unfortunately, words lack so much when it comes to feelings. What I will say is that if I could bottle how I feel I would be a multi-billionaire overnight, and the shops would be in demand for an eternity.

Right, big words I know, so let's get on with it. I apologise for any poor English or writing skills as I'm no writer, I never have been, but I can't just sit on what I have been shown, and so wrote this book over a period of around 3 years in the hope it strikes a chord of truth with you the reader, either confirming what you already believe or changing your belief structure regarding the reality of 'what is'. Let's begin!

Chapter 1

A Little About Me.

I entered this world on the 22nd of February 1975, and was born into the land of the seventies English council estate. Dad was never there, but I was blessed with a lovely mother and two older brothers with more than enough love to give, life was good and was as challenging as anyone else's life. I was raised as part of a big loving family, a family to be proud of. I'm not going to delve into my childhood as there's no point, however I will say that my childhood was very challenging. I feel that this is important to tell you the reader because I believe my particular character has led me to this unique journey into insight, self-discovery and truth.

I'm a very deep and loving soul, and I have always been inquisitive, and since I can remember I have always, it seems, been obsessed with truth. I was always the child in class that asked the stupid question (well at the time I was certainly given the feeling that my question was stupid). This feeling was not just conveyed by my school friends but also by the teacher; a teacher that usually never even attempted an answer, but a teacher that usually looked at me funny and laughed it off as though I'd never asked the question to begin with. I did have a teacher that was honest enough to answer me once, an A-level Organic Chemistry Teacher, and he laughingly replied, "I've never been asked the questions you ask me, and I have gone home and tried to find you answers and I can't."

Looking back this made me realise two things; the first was that the teachers and the text books did not know the answers to everything, and the second lesson I have since learned is that my questions as strange as they may have been to my friends, were in fact not strange at all. The truth was that the teacher laughed because it was easier to laugh than to admit the truth. The truth was that the teacher did not know the answer, and found it easier to pass off his own inadequacy as a fault of my own.

It is clear now on reflection that I was not strange at all, my thinking was simply a little different. I knew at a very early age that my soul, spirit and whole self was very different to my friends and peers at school.

Anyway, with my ever-investigative brain in full swing and after years of beating myself up for feeling so different, I slowly over time, a long and difficult time began to embrace the person I was and still am today.

Our soul, the essence of what we truly are never changes. We may over time forget our 'true self' and hide with invisible masks and ego charades, but the essence of the 'true self' never changes, and can in time with the right conditions become revealed again.

Once I decided to give myself up to that what I have always been, my life seemed to open up before me. I began a journey, an outward journey of seeking the truth to the questions I needed answering, and not the questions school had once imposed on me. The questions I wanted answering were; why are we here? Are there aliens out there in the vast cosmos of our Universe? Do ghosts exist? Is clairvoyance real? And the two biggest questions for me, and equally as baffling as the questions prior were; what is my purpose? (I always felt I had a job to do yet had no idea what it was). The other big question was, 'What's it all about?' And why was I constantly engaged in a conversation with God, and why was my belief so strong in an entity that was void in my house growing up, and in the environment around me?

I'm a white working class male, and where I grew

up people didn't talk about God. My mother chose to give us the choice to make up our own minds regarding God, religion etc. In fact, the only strong conversation I ever heard regarding God was between my mother and a very tearful uncle of mine when my nan passed away. The conversation was more like a screaming conclusion when I heard my uncle shout, "God doesn't exist, how could he when my mom has died!".

    Naturally even though I was very young at the time I did understand his pain; this was my nan and I loved her dearly, yet this was his mom, he was 18 and she was gone. All this however had little effect if any on my love and belief of our creator. The answers to these questions, 'what was my purpose?' And 'what's it all about?' Could not be found outwardly, an inner journey of self-discovery had to also take place.

    I know this now, after many years of inner discovery and acceptance of myself. I tried the outward search for God and the obvious route was religion, however it saddens me to say that the God I was seeking, was the creator of everything, a God that transcended religious belief. A God that was free from a particular set of opinions and doctrines.

    Here was my problem with religion. All religious belief systems seemed to be saying similar things, like that there was a beginning point or a creation point, and all religions seemed to have parts within them that rang true. My problem with religion was that if you belong to a certain religious group you straight away stand in opposition of other belief systems, because to validate your own particular belief sometimes means negating anything that comes from a different source, and this saddened me. How can you just have blind faith? I understand a search for God but to accept blindly and negate all other paths sadly for myself displayed ignorance.

Here is a question to anyone that follows a particular belief; if you are a Christian and have total faith in your religion and not just God alone, would you be any different if you had been born into a Muslim country with a Muslim family? I would happily gamble that the answer would be no. My point is that a simple turn of destiny could have put you in direct contrast to where you are now, and yet quite probably you would have the same faith but instead be praising from a new perspective. If you were born in Pakistan and wanted God, you would probably be pointed in the direction of the mosque. In England if you asked where you could find God, you would be pointed to the church. But you could also equally be pointed to the mosque or temple as well.

My point is simple; to stand in a box of confinement limits your own learning and understanding. I know if you sought God then quite possibly you would try to find our creator in a church, a mosque, a temple in fact any of these buildings, I have never gone to church or a mosque to find God. I've always found a closeness to God in more natural places, like looking at the sun go down whilst sitting on a beach, or whilst watering my flowers in my garden, as I look at the splendour and beauty of the world around me. I don't negate religion, I love anyone that displays the true essence of any religion. The simple values, 'don't judge', 'love one another', be of 'good intention'. These values are simple and when lived out in full the world becomes a more beautiful place to be.

I have friends from all walks of life, both believers and nonbelievers, and the ones closest to me are the ones that display these values at heart, regardless of their particular race or belief. These are good people. So therefore, what I sought could not be found in one particular religion.

In stark contrast to religion and despite a popular belief that science has no place with God, I discovered the force behind the conversation I had had since childhood in places you are told God has no place, within the realm of science. Also, it seems that God can be found in the closest place to all of us, hidden deep within us, right at the centre of your entire being...your consciousness. But we will discuss this later.

For the rest of this book I will at times refer to God as the 'Universal consciousness'. This term will make much more sense later.

Anyway, as a child growing up I was forever analysing situations, people around me, and even myself. I was 'self-aware' at a very young age. When I use the term 'self-aware' I mean that from around 4 or 5 I knew my actions had an effect on others and on the world around me.

Looking back, it is very clear that this seeking of truth both outwardly and inwardly was and is a big part of my life. I now love the way in which I look into myself and the world around me.

How can you ever grow and develop as a person if you do not know yourself? And not just the good parts of you but the bad as well. And 'how can you ever find truth if you do not seek it yourself?' It is impossible.

If you were a truly competitive athlete aiming to achieve your best then you would be aware of your weaknesses, because with the awareness of the faults you can fix the problems. In doing so the athlete becomes a better version of his or her prior self. Yet as humans we seldom do this. Instead most times, rather than look at ourselves and what effect our actions cause in our lives, we point the finger of blame outwardly. Looking for someone else to blame when life doesn't work out how we want. Yet from day one it is our choices that bring rewards either good or bad.

Looking inwards is a beautiful and at times can be, a very scary journey. Looking outwards is very much the same. You can look at the world and see suffering, war, disease and general global chaos which at times is very scary, but like the journey inwards the outward journey can be beautiful, for example when was the last time you sat in the middle of nowhere, fields as far as the eye can see, breathing in natures air; air as fresh on the lungs as nature had intended it? Or simply marvelled at a flower with the summer sun on your face?

This was and is my journey, however with this outlook towards truth, and seeing things as they truly are and without any prior prejudice or judgement can bring with it one major drawback, and that is that when you see the world truthfully you quickly realise it is both beautiful and at the same time it's not a very nice place at all. There were naturally for me growing up days of love, days of sadness, days of happiness and days of loneliness.

I was outwardly social but internally there was always a conflict. It is hard to pinpoint exact feelings after so long but I remember having a massive feeling of being 'out of place'. I also seemed to draw the attention of the school bully quite a lot, (I must have seemed an easy target). As a child, we had moved houses a few times and although we stayed around the same area I had to move schools because of distance. This moving from school to school slowly made me become a little withdrawn from the person I was deep down.

I had been raised in the local borough's rough estate so from an early age I was fighting, not through choice, I had to. The late seventies and early eighties were like that. I can remember my mom making me fight on a couple of occasions, purely for the reason of making me stick up for myself. Like I said earlier my dad wasn't around so my mom did the best she could to raise myself and my brothers in a way she believed a man would have done if one had been about the house.

So, fighting was in the fabric of the society I grew up in. And up to the age of about 11, I had participated in excess of around 12-13 fist fights. This isn't a good thing at all and it's a sad reflection of society at that time, I mention it just to let you know that I was never afraid of the battle of life growing up (you simply did not have a choice). Not the initial years anyway sadly in my teens my attitude had changed and all of a sudden I seemed to become withdrawn and I had become scared; scared of what I do not know, but genuinely scared. Bullies would get in my face and I would freeze, naturally this led other bullies that had heard I wasn't fighting back to also stand in front of me and try and get me to fight. I can remember lying in bed at night crying myself to sleep, not out of fear, but because I was ashamed of myself, ashamed that I hadn't fought back.

Over time the old me started to come back, and in my late teens I began training in martial arts. This interest and love came into my life at just the right time. I had always been fascinated by Heroes and also Eastern culture. My hero growing up was Bruce Lee, and I had always been drawn to the mystical nature of Eastern culture that seemed to project out of early 70's T.V. and movies. I would sit avidly and watch the T.V. show Kung Fu, and I would totally lose my mind when I watched the Chinese T.V. show Monkey; which usually culminated in me chopping and kicking invisible enemies in my living room then calling my pink cloud to jump on and fly away (you would have had to have watched it!).

This fascination early in life must have opened the

door to spirituality and to the philosophy of mind, body and spirit being one. As long as I could remember I had been drawn towards Eastern culture. And now martial arts would become my vessel of learning. It had such an impact that martial arts would consume the next 17 years of my life.

Towards the end of my teens I had begun to like the person I was. There were still huge holes in my life, and so many things I simply did not understand, and my question remained unanswered, what was my purpose? This was the big one, because I had no idea of what I wanted to do once I had left school.

I've loved drawing and painting since my early childhood, but I had no idea which way to go with it, and so not really knowing what I wanted to do once I finished my A-levels, I went on to university to study chemistry. This was a bad decision, but one made after talking to a family member, an uncle whom I love dearly and that shared my passion for Art and more specifically portrait art.

My uncle had advised me that making money from Art was hard to do, and that most Artists made more money after they had died. With this information absorbed I quickly chose another course at university. I think I lasted one year on the chemistry course before it dawned on me that this was wrong.

I don't blame my uncle for this at all, this is what we all do for love. We try to help our family with advice based on our own ideas of what we know.

More than ever I was feeling that I was in the wrong place, and that more was meant for me. Over the next couple of years, I tried my hand at a few varied careers, I will try and recall them in order but there were quite a lot, so here goes; retail sales, barman, food factory operative, nightclub barman and nightclub promotions, and then it seemed out of nowhere and with no foresight or planning I was the lead dancer and choreographer in a 70's themed comedy stage show!

This path had literally manifested itself from one creative fuelled conversation between myself and the General Manager of one of the West Midlands' leading commercial nightclubs. He had originally employed me as a barman and quickly we had struck up a friendship; I was in my early twenties and my friend was in his early forties and a very successful club manager, we would finish work at this huge commercial night spot and then we would head out to what we called 'Clubland', the House music scene in and around the West Midlands.

Anyone that was fortunate enough to be a part of the 90's club scene will remember just how great that era was. Our particular favourite clubbing spots could be found in and around Birmingham; epic nights with licensing laws that meant at 2am all the alcohol drinkers usually went home, leaving a venue full of likeminded speed and ecstasy fuelled individuals, dancing in their own particular bubble. Once the dancing ended you usually ended up chatting to a complete stranger about how great the music was, or just share how fantastic you may have felt at that time.

On one particular evening of clubbing, myself and the club manager were chatting about what new things we could bring to the club where we both worked. Out of this conversation came the creation of our comedy stage show, based on fictional 70's characters that would come out and engage the crowd, dancing along to 70's disco dance floor fillers. It would be led by Dick Shaft, a fictional porn star, star of the movies 'The Sperminator' and 'Around the world in 80 lays', and so the 70's porn legend was born, and I was wearing his white trousers and shiny platform shoes!

I loved my job, for the first time ever I felt like I was free, free to create, to create in the choreography (even though I had never danced), to create my own character and to create extra characters for the show and to dress and style these characters. I was very happy and I can't recall ever really not wanting to go to work. Sadly, I knew this still was not what I was meant to be doing, even though it bought me a glimmer of happiness and for a while a little stability. However, I was 21 and still felt as though this was not where I was meant to be.

You could not ask for more really, I was young, dancing in clubs that on some nights would have up to 3500 people in them. One nightclub we were a part of was having our show broadcast out on radio every Thursday evening, and once I even recall driving down the M6 to Coventry and hearing a discussion on the radio about Dick Shaft. Sadly, even though I was 'living the life', deep down I was still on a spiritual level not happy. I was happy enough though to live this life for 4 years, and this career led me to meet the mother of my son. I mention this because there are times in our lives that we do not understand, I wasn't truly happy being a dancer even though I loved the role and yet out of these few years came my son, so in hindsight it wasn't wasted time, in fact it was a very productive period in the story of my life.

Shortly afterwards I joined the country's leading male dance act, and yet despite being offered several T.V. opportunities I walked away from it all to join the Army.

The reasons I joined the Army were quite simple but so very wrong regarding me finding my happiness on a spiritual level, I was planning to settle down with the mother of my child and I needed stability and a career. I had nothing really to show since leaving school to any employer that was going to be of any interest to anyone looking to employ an apprentice tradesperson, or someone wanting to learn a trade. I just kept getting the same response which was, "Why do you want a trade when you were a dancer for 4 years. Why not dance?"

I was getting nowhere fast so one day whilst I was walking past the Army careers centre in Wolverhampton I decided to pop in and take a look. A few weeks later I was sat in a room about to receive the results of my test; a test called the BARB test, based on logic, English and maths and how quickly it is completed.

A very happy uniformed man entered the room to inform me that I had just scored the highest score ever on their system since the careers centre had opened. I was chuffed to say the least and was offered several options which were Officer training at Sandhurst; they offered this based on my Barb score and based on me having A-levels and having gone to university. They also offered me the Intelligence Corp and the Royal Military Police.

After going home and chatting with my then partner I decided to go into the Royal Military Police and shortly afterwards did so. I began 'Basic Training', which was 14 weeks spent away from home, in the beautiful picturesque city of Winchester. The Army Training Regiment of Winchester was my home during the winter of 2000. Army training was amazing, and the friends of my platoon became my family for the following months.

I was a keen learner and I am proud to say that on our 'Passing Out Parade' I received the award for 'Best shot' of my platoon. After 'Passing out' (a term given that means completing basic training) from 8 Windsor platoon I went home on leave and began to realise that although I was loving army life, and loving the challenges both physically and mentally, I was still spiritually very unhappy. And the everlasting question of what my purpose was, was still very much unanswered and I was getting a little concerned that I might never find out what it was. Once this seed of doubt had been planted it quickly blossomed and culminated in me shortly afterwards leaving the army.

The 12 months that followed were a strange combination of incredible happiness and a melancholic darkness centred around the fact I was lost inside, and for the first time ever I had no goal to work towards. I had truly lost myself within this game of life. Here I was on one hand about to marry my partner, and yet on the other hand I was lost, my relationship had become poisoned from within by a darkness my partner at the time was carrying, this darkness had through both our actions begun to cloud my life, I was smothered and had no sense of self, or direction and the long-lost question of purpose had no chance of ever being answered, not where I was. I was married and shortly afterwards became a father to my whole world, my lovely son.

Within a year of my son being born my relationship with his mother was quickly breaking down and eventually the darkness of those around had caught up with me and I had to do something because things were just too bad to be a part of. I never just upped and left, I was put into a situation where I simply had no other choice, I had to go.

I don't know if you the reader have any children, but when you have them the last thing you want to do is scream or shout or allow them to witness violence between their parents. I did not want my son to be around a situation like that and so after a very violent row one afternoon I left, and filed for divorce the following day, as well as see a solicitor to arrange contact for myself to see my son.

I was 27 years old and living in a garage at my mom's house. I had been accused of everything by my ex in an attempt to stop me seeing my son. I was awaiting a divorce and fighting a custody battle for my son as well as countless other allegations placed upon me. I was tired and desperately missing him and the only outlet I had for my pain was the gym, martial arts and working security every weekend in various nightclubs for cash and as a way to get all the frustrations life was placing upon me, out.

This period of my life was the darkest I have ever had and I hope that nobody ever that has done nothing wrong is put in a position where they cannot see their child. Not seeing your child is like living with grief for a departed loved one, the only difference being is that they are alive and well and wondering where the hell their parents are and missing you in equal measure.

All through my life I had been interested in and participated in martial arts and the gym. I was 28 years old and still had no sense of purpose, what I did have was a ton of negative energy, and nowhere to release it. It is a hard path to remain calm and civil when you are being accused of all sorts of nonsense by your former Wife. A woman you've shared the experience of creating a child with, a woman that suddenly becomes hostile and because of their partners wishes tries their hardest to deny you access to your child. I was very quickly training for 4 hours every day, training martial arts as well as hitting the gym hard, pushing weights. All of this just being a diversion from life and the pains I was carrying at that time.

Looking back, it is clear now why I was so active. I couldn't face the pain, it was too much, I missed my son. So, to take my mind of issues during periods where I needed to remain patient (the months waiting for court dates etc.), I submerged myself into my training. I was periodically, day in day out beating the hell out of myself in the gym. Always pushing further and further as this was the biggest and healthiest distraction I could find. Alcohol was not an option, neither was adopting a party lifestyle. My intention was good (even though the battle was slowly destroying me inside, outwardly I was getting stronger and stronger), I knew one day I would see my son again, deep down I had faith in the fact I had done nothing wrong and massive faith that once the court system saw things for themselves then they would quickly allow contact between myself and my son to begin. Therefore, I could not allow what I was going through to destroy me, I had no intention of my son seeing a broken version of his dad. My son was going to see me again and I was going to be stronger, bigger and showing no signs of being broken.

  The gym and martial arts environment quickly led me into the club game again, this time as a Doorman (the man in the black suit responsible for making sure adults behave in a respectable manner to one another when intoxicated). This was not the perfect place to vent negative energy, and is one of the worst environments to ever 'lose it'. A cloud of darkness had descended all around me, a veil so thick and black that I will never forget that period of my life. I was thrust into a dark place and whilst there I chose a negative way to deal with negative problems.

  Yes, I was doing everything right regarding jumping through the various 'hoops' my ex had set up for me in an attempt to stop me seeing my boy. I had not seen my son in almost 6 months and this was not through my own choice. There were forces at work that were well and truly trying their hardest to destroy me and my relationship with my son.

  Behind the stage of the court system I was angry, and getting increasingly unstable. A good doorman friend of mine had given me the nickname 'Sandman', because of how many men I had put to sleep using my jiu-jitsu training whilst working the doors. All these men were at the time either trying to hurt a customer, hurt a colleague or trying to hurt myself. The term 'hurt' I use loosely, on the doors I encountered everything from fists whizzing past my jaw, to dodging bottles and ducking baseball bats. It was a very active Nightclub, the friend that gave me this nickname later went on to fight in the world's leading MMA organisation, so I was keeping good company and making myself a bit of a name. This was not good though and karma as they say, is a bitch!

Eventually this negative approach caught me up, resulting in a massive punch-up outside the nightspot I worked at, on an evening I wasn't even working! The people whoever they were that had started the trouble that evening was insignificant, what was significant was that I was falling apart.

I've always tried my hardest to do things right in life and had always managed to hold myself together, but not this time. I exploded! The pain of not seeing my son was getting more painful by the day, as the lies and deceit from the other side were starting to take their toll. Finally, I gave way and all the anger, frustration and emotion all came tumbling out. Thankfully this happened in my work life and luckily didn't lead to any consequences in my home life.

Naturally these events were all building towards a destruction of myself. My defining moment I guess came at my lowest point. All I remember is that one night I was in an emotional mess. I'd vented physically, there was no doubt about that. It is strange, but after withstanding massive attempts from my ex to break me, it was in fact the smallest of things that sent me tipping over the edge. Sending me skidding off the straight and narrow, and straight down Destruction Avenue.

    I remember sliding down my wall at home; the posters and photos tearing away from their fixings as my heavy body slid toward the floor catching screws and pins on the way down, tears pouring down my face, feeling lost and empty, missing my only child, my son, my son I love and adore. I remember having a thought, a very bad thought...the 'easy way out' thought.

    I was deep in a hole, the deepest that anyone could be in, and then something strange occurred, I heard a voice from within, a voice that was familiar but one I had never heard before. A voice that was so soft, a beautiful tone, a voice armed with the right words to lift me to my feet again. I had never in all my life heard God speak so clearly, not before or since, and the words were simply, "Get up."

    I had hit the lowest point in my life, I had battled to do what was right, always having the inner belief that doing the right thing would naturally help me see my son again. The voice inside said few words, and yet it resounded so strong and loud that my whole life and what I stand for came to the front of my mind and thankfully I listened to that voice. It could have all ended right there and then, the story of my life. I was messed up, lost and torn apart on my bedroom floor. Instead I chose to fight and that moment saved my life. I came away from working in the nightclub scene at that point and decided to take a step back. I was confused, and in a dark place. I decided to go out and buy a piano, some canvasses and paints, and I began painting again, something I had not done in over 9 years.

    I can thank my mom for this. All through my life she has been there, supportive and helpful at times of need, and for that alone I know that I am blessed. Somehow what I had lacked in a father I had gained in a mother that truly went the extra mile for her children. And in true super-mom fashion it was she that asked me a simple question the day I received the call from the head of the door firm asking me to take some time off. The question was simple, "What do you want to do kid?"

And my answer was clearer than it had ever been, I had just walked back from the gates of hell, picked myself up and brushed myself down. And so, with a clarity like never before I decided that I had run for so long from what I had always loved, and with what I had been through I felt nothing could scare me away, I wanted to paint. Regardless of what I had heard about Artists being poor and few making it, I knew that this is what had made me happy as a child, and that this was what I was going to pursue.

Putting down my Door supervisor badge and picking up a paintbrush literally saved my life. Time has passed by now, and the darkness with lots of small steps has been eradicated and replaced with light.

And now here I am sitting in the sun on an early English spring morning, 13 years have passed since that evening. I'm taking a break with my family, my new partner, her child and my son, almost 14 years old. My son that lives with me full time. My love for him has no boundaries, a love so strong that when he wasn't in my life it nearly destroyed me, but a love so strong that rather than destroy me, it gave me the courage, the stamina and the strength to fight on.

I'm currently 'Glamping', a modern-day camping experience. As I sit here and type away, there are ducks all around our safari tent. The sun is shining and the air is as fresh as nature intended it to be. This is heaven. Since that dark evening, I won full custody of my son, rediscovered my 'true self' and went back to university and graduated with Honours in Fine Art and began living again.

I now run my own business and have even higher hopes than those which I've already achieved. I am more than happy to say that my business actually revolves around my passion for Art. I'm a Tattoo Fine Artist, my studio is fully booked and I get to be creative every day, and at long last I feel purpose, a true purpose.

I love life, love and cherish every moment that I have. I love the simple things, I appreciate the warmth of the sun on my cheeks, sit in wonder as bird's land around the pond in my garden at home. I stop now when I see something beautiful in the world around me, rather than pass it by in the hurry of life. Why? Well because I've seen the pit, I've been rock bottom and I've lived in the darkness.

I truly know that to see and fully appreciate the light we have to stand in the darkness. There's a light in all of us and how bright it burns depends on us and us alone. We all have it deep within us. A light so bright it can change our lives, change our thoughts and ultimately change our own unique reality and Universe.

This life, this world and this Universe is far too complex to ever truly comprehend and understand, and yet the universes greatest gift is its simplicity. A simplicity that through modern day education and fast paced living becomes drowned out. You have a purpose, a passion uniquely your own, something no one else can ever do like you, and when you do find it, nurture it, protect it and fight for it!

The rewards will naturally come, for those things we do that we love, we ultimately do well, and through patience and dedication we can master, and even achieve a level of skill never seen before. Anything done to that level will be sought after, and the riches will follow.

I now know my purpose, and following this path

has made me the richest man on earth, as I possess something money cannot buy and that is peace of mind. I wake now already happy and when the day is done I can put my head to my pillow and sleep with no difficulty. In the past when I was lost and unsure I would dread bed time. As soon as my head would hit the pillow every nagging question and doubt in life would come crashing in, resulting in a very restless night's sleep. I know I keep saying it but we all should find our own unique purpose. Our purpose is important.

Everything has a purpose, there is nothing that has ever been created that has no purpose. If a single cellular organism has a purpose, and a tree has a purpose, and a star has a purpose then logic clearly suggests that a highly organised multi cellular conscious being such as a human would have a purpose. And since we have free choice (well free choice if we choose consciously), then logic again suggests that all our purposes are as infinitely different to one another's in an infinite outcome of possibilities.

This explains why the universal question of 'what is it all about?' Has never been answered. There is it seems a purpose to us as a whole, as in everything in the known universe, but there is naturally no desire or plan in place that would make us all have the same purpose. Our overall purpose as a species is naturally a lot different to our own unique purpose as an individual. In later chapters, we will discuss how you can begin the journey to discover your true self and purpose, and discuss the purpose of the Universe and how our unique purpose reflects God and the Universal consciousness, and answer the question, 'what is it all about?' Even though our purposes are very different the point of life is the same for all; our own actions and thoughts help the Universal consciousness God, evolve. Whether we contribute positively or negatively is down to us.

When I was a child I always spoke to a higher force on a daily basis, but later in life I'd started to blank things out and the conversation and belief had started to diminish. When I was fighting to see my son, I found the conversation between myself and the Universe had begun once again, this conversation was usually me asking for guidance and strength.

At 33 I felt that I had finally found my true purpose, or at least part of it. It had been a long journey but it was complete, a discovery of what I am. And through this self-analysis and seeking of truth, a journey began, a journey of 'self-discovery'. A true 'self-discovery', a discovery from deep within that I know I am a part of something much bigger. This will all be shared.

During my own unique journey, I began to notice that there were unseen forces at work trying to get my attention. Needless to say, this force was greater than myself and indeed in time it did succeed. And a new conversation began, however this conversation was different to all the others I had ever had, this time I was standing with a different perspective, a perspective of purpose and of knowing. And this time I was not asking for guidance, or help or strength. In fact, I was not asking at all, I was having my usual daily conversation with the Universe, just being thankful for what I had got. I had got a break in a career I had thought about and longed to do when I was 18, but had been told was impossible, as back then opportunities in this career were rare, very rare, so deep down I had kind of given up.

So, I was in a happy place and I certainly wasn't seeking any kind of distractions, I knew what I wanted and I was determined to stay on the right path to one day achieve my goals. Winning my son had taught me that, all through the custody battle I remained calm and behaved with dignity (in the courts and at home) despite having a thousand and one accusations thrown at me. Yes, karma may have dealt its hand in my work life where I was taking out all the pain of not seeing my son, but karma also dealt its hand regarding my son, and after doing everything right and never rising to the attempts to provoke me from the other side, I eventually was granted a weekend contact order. Within months the courts had a dramatic turnaround due to events in my ex-partner's life and I was awarded full custody.

 So, the door of karma clearly swings both ways.

This conversation with God or the 'Universal consciousness' was different, as it was as though the Universe had something to show me, and it did. This dialect as crazy as it sounds, as enabled me to meet new friends, some that I have never even spoken to face to face, some alive and some long gone from this earth, but like minded individuals that have shared their truths, truths that seem to resonate for all time.

I've been given information along my journey, information that is not new, information that has been spoken before, yet information I know you have probably never heard. Information that when you hear it, will resonate truth and resonate an understanding. All I want to do is share what I have found with you. Open your mind, sit back and take in what you are about to read. Do not just accept it as fact, see what rings true instead.

Truth is where your dreams reside, if you can't be truthful about your life and the person you are then you will never grow to your fullest potential, and never realise your purpose. If you can release what is within you, then it will save you. If you do not, then what is within you will slowly destroy you.

You are here at this point in your life because of every choice and decision you have ever made. If you're in a bad place it is through your own choices. If you are in a good place, then again that will without doubt be because of the choices you have made. This is the Universal Law of 'cause and effect'. Many will sit right now and still read this and blame life circumstances etc. for their own short comings in life. Life will naturally have its pain such as death, and also its rewards such as the birth of a child. The position from where we experience these trials from however depends ultimately on our own choices up to and including that point.

Don't feel defensive if you've made poor decisions because here is the truth, and for most people it is a very difficult pill to swallow, most of your choices have never really been your own conscious choices. It is the programming of the unconscious mind that can govern most of your choices. And it is this programming you first need to release in order to live consciously and finally make choices that are truly your own.

Once you begin to live consciously every day, you slowly open your mind and spirit and the Universal consciousness and its secrets become revealed. It is here you will find purpose, find understanding of what is and begin a conversation with your creator.

Let's begin....

Chapter 2

The Mind Trap.

So, you wake up, wash your face, brush your teeth, have breakfast and face the world. The world you face while you're having your breakfast usually comes in the form of some rushed family morning time combined with at some point the world or local news, mostly negative with the odd hint of cheer emanating from the square box in the living room, pumping out a plethora of negativity for you to soak up before you've even left your house to begin the day, and if this isn't your chosen method of soaking up what's going on in the world well then there is always the daily newspapers, as well as an array of social media sites for you to get your negative energy fix and mass media brain washing from.

So, with this negativity planted into your brain you begin the working day. And that is if you're lucky, because there are a lot of people that wake everyday feeling empty, jobless, homeless, and even suicidal.

However most set off for work driven by their own individual goals, 'Are the bills paid?' 'Can I afford the holiday coming up?' 'Are my mortgage repayments going to be paid this month?' These are just a handful of some of the questions and problems we face every day, and are merely examples. What is the importance of such trivial matters that block up and consume our very thoughts? What is the purpose? Because continuous time wasted dwelling on these life challenges leads to no end result other than grinding you down slowly over your short time that you get to spend here.

The purpose of all life's time consuming thoughts to cope with the grind of life is simple; it is there to busy you and pull your conscious mind into a state of worrying or thinking either of yesterday and what may have happened or to worry about future events that quite simply haven't happened yet, and sadly this frame of mind serves you no purpose at all. The importance? Again, these are of no real importance either, well not to you, unless you enjoy spending your entire working life chasing some pot of gold at the end of a rainbow that doesn't exist.

It is a true and sad fact that all of it, all the media, all the news, all the T.V. programming is orchestrated, all the systematic hum drum soul consuming monotonous chores we do. You are free, although hopelessly enslaved by a fear driven social conditioning that trains your mindset to compete continually with your peers for more money, nicer cars, nicer homes, nicer clothes, a mindset that conditions you that you're merely a material being, a mindset that conditions you to accept the truth that they the 'system' deem as the truth, whilst all the time missing the big picture which is you're not actually free, you are controlled, controlled eloquently by this mindset, the mindset that from an early age has been conditioned to accept the world around them and to question very little, a mindset that has separated you from your 'true self'.

The truth is we're all hopelessly enslaved to this system, no one is truly free, but we do have the choice to decide how much we allow the global mindset to condition us, and it is here we can choose freedom, but only by engaging our conscious mind, for the unconscious mind chooses actions based on previous experience, therefore this state offers no real choice. We must maintain an engaged consciousness to truly make informed decisions.

There is a fate much worse than being enslaved to this 'merry go round' called life, and that is riding the 'merry go round' and believing you're there because it is all you deserve, and much worse believing that you can't step off this ride and change things. You can, and you always could.

    The only purpose that this lifestyle leads to is that it increases the profit margins of the banks and anyone else who is a part of the corporate machine. It serves you no purpose at all, unless you base your ideals on materialism that is, and even then, most likely these material items will still be a struggle to obtain. Take a look at the profit margins of the global leaders in commercial fashion and sports retail goods. Take a look at the bonuses these managing directors of multinational companies receive. The system is thriving at the very top, yet it would collapse if you the consumer, or you the corporate worker chose a different outlook, an outlook of truth to oneself rather than the truth of whatever it is the masses are doing at this time. It is this reason as well as many others that the powers that be instil a conditioned mindset. A mindset so conditioned it drives the gears of the corporate global machine.

    What is unfortunate is that as individuals we are programmed to follow the masses, and the masses make up the biggest percentage of our society. It is the largest part of society that unfortunately do not succeed financially in a way that could set them up for life. Society is not set up so that the strong fail, it seems to be set up so that the weak survive. There is a lower level of existence available to everyone, that does suit less motivated individuals. A system that ensures long working hours for a minimum wage, a wage that low the individual has to work long hours just to maintain a very simple life. It seems fair, it is hardly testing for an individual to adopt this simple form of minimal effort existence.

And yet anyone who walks this path of minimal effort will in no time discover a sad truth. That being that this path is probably the hardest one of all. It will take away your choices, your free time, your family time, and will probably take away your life a whole lot quicker than what you had expected. And the alternative to this life?... a life created by you, an existence that walks forward with the world, an existence that creates both positive change in their own reality and in the world around them. An existence free from dogmatic thinking, an existence where you are truly you.

While you are accepting blindly and riding this system you're probably unaware of how much you have been brainwashed. This is a system that teaches us from an early age with the school system to accept information presented from a higher authority as fact, and not to question it, is this not dangerous? Is this all we really want from our minds? Do we really want our minds conditioned to just accept? Because that is what is happening to our children. And it was how you were taught and your parents and grandparents before them.

Just for a moment take yourself back into the classroom and relive your school days, the child that questioned what was being taught, and perhaps asked the mind-expanding questions usually got ridiculed by the class or teacher. Like mentioned in the previous chapter regarding my own life experience. There will naturally be exceptions to the rule, but some teachers will, due to time restraints and a lack of total understanding of the subject being taught, be unable to give a reasonable answer, and instead shut the student off.

And yet it is totally fair and just to say that the child that blindly accepts the facts and then regurgitates them for an exam will succeed, the more the child accepts these facts the better their exam results will be and hence the true blind fact absorbers gain the best results in their respective school exams.

What happens next? Well these children go on to get the jobs and careers in the highest positions within society. They become politicians, police officers, social workers, bankers, government workers and in some cases teachers.

Why is this wrong? It is wrong for one reason, and one reason only. Let us be honest we want the children that are the brightest to grow up and gain the jobs in the highest positions within society, or do we? Is this all we want? Just look at society now and consider how many things within it that are wrong.

Since you were a child have any of the major issues around global affairs been resolved? Let's consider a few of the biggest world issues today; war, famines and disease within some parts of Africa, and Global warming. These issues could not get any bigger, we are talking in all three examples about death. In war, the death of many and not just soldiers, but innocents also, including children. In Africa, the death of millions maybe billions over the years so far, either through famine or disease. Diseases curable with cheap modern day medicine, yet quite simply out of the reach to these people because of the cost. A continent ravaged and broken down by the West in the form of slavery over 200 years ago, a time that took most of the male population away. And still 200 years on people wonder why areas clearly still struggle even today to get the simplest of things, simple things like water.

And in the final example we are talking death, not of a few but maybe of an entire species, or the total eradication of all life as we know it, if things do not change. And this is not by any means an over exaggeration.

We're depleting massive amounts of the Amazon rain forest and countless others worldwide, and it is both naive and stupid to believe that ripping acres upon acres of trees down will bear little effect to our eco-system. The destruction of the rain forest is only one example of how we as man, the apex species on this our own home Earth, choose to destroy with little thought of the consequence to later generations, our planet.

Fortunately, we will never destroy the planet, an asteroid hitting Earth that wiped out the dinosaurs completely could not alter Earth's life creating capabilities, but we can easily wipe ourselves out. We rely on certain conditions to survive and thrive on this planet, and with great sadness, our actions are quickly changing the conditions we so dearly need.

So, going back to the question of, 'why is it wrong that the blind fact absorbers go on to get the highest jobs within society?' We have had this system for centuries now and nothing is really changing. Nothing is changing at all. Parts of Africa still struggle and will always struggle with famines and disease, the trees are still being ripped down globally to produce paper, and at some point, we will if things do not change, reach a point of no return with the damage on our own eco system, resulting in ultimately man's battle for existence, as well as many other species battling for their own survival too. This is wrong, and this is selfish. Would it not be more beneficial to society as a whole if we had these clever sharp minded children taught to question at school and not just to accept? Imagine how insightful and creative these minds would be. Minds that were free enough to accept and question current paper producing methods used globally and seek safer alternatives, because there are safer alternatives out there to be explored. Or the insightful child that grows up to become a politician and is creative enough to raise the question of why parts of Africa have been abandoned with little effort to remedy the problem and yet for other countries (countries that seem to function without famine or disease but maybe contain an oil source), we have as a nation donned our army uniforms and gone in heavy handed to protect the people?!

We need society to change, and the only way to create change in our society is to begin to teach our children not just facts, but how to be themselves and how to question. Encourage them to be creative in their thinking, and not to ever feel bad in any sense for questioning at all. Unfortunately, the powers that be do not wish for you to question, because in questioning you start to discover the truth, and when you start to see the world around you with truth framed glasses you begin to see just how orchestrated to serve just a few it is. If we do nothing and just blindly be conditioned then the circle of the blindly indoctrinated leading the blind to be indoctrinated continues, all riding a merry go round of facts, facts that teach us how to not be uniquely ourselves, facts that teach us not to think but to remember, teaching us to become spoon fed by the information the system wants you to receive.

If you believe that I am wrong then please quickly try and remember how many things you were taught at school that were fact, that later on were changed with new research and new discoveries. For example, I got taught at school that Pluto was the 9th planet and back then it was definitely a fact! Remember you can't question the teacher so it had to be a fact. Quite recently Pluto was declassified from being a planet, and was later classified as a Kuiper belt object. So, a few years ago, things changed and we had 8 planets and lots of rocky Kuiper belt objects and that became fact. Just recently planets have been discovered outside of the Kuiper belt, which has led scientists to the conclusion that there is still no certain definite number as regards to the number of planets in our solar system. This is one example of facts being wrong with later studies, and there are many more, the point I am trying to make here is that outside of the teaching of maths, science and a few other subjects, there are no facts. There are only current theories and opinions. And yet the school system repeatedly teaches, then tests their pupils' responses based on the repetition of the facts given. No points in a test being given to the child that maybe hypothesised that there were possibly more planets out there, just maybe beyond our reach at that current time.

  We want our children to know facts but we should encourage them to be able to think outside of the box as well. A mind that takes current ideas regarding absolutely anything and takes whatever it may be to another level. There is nothing in this world that does not have its root of creation in thought. We need to let down the restrictive barriers our schools and social circles place within our mind, to see the real truth, only then will we begin to use our minds to their fullest potential.

  We are the only creatures on this planet that can manifest into reality our thoughts. For example, if I imagine a garden shed in my mind with windows, a door and a felt roof, then from that thought I may make a sketch that later becomes a more detailed plan to carry out the sheds construction. My initial thought has now manifested into reality. This is why a free mind is needed to transcend what has become normal day current society. We truly have the minds strong enough to manifest the changes needed in today's world, not just for us but for future generations also.

  To teach ourselves and our children to open up and

use every part of our brain is truly the key to change. We are not meant to be programmed like computers. It was us that invented the computer. Our minds have such great potential, and that potential becomes limited when it is conditioned to just accept fact after fact. Our minds need to learn facts and hold information, but we also need enquiry, to question, to delve, to seek, it is the way we were created. And it plays the ultimate role in the evolution of the Universe as a whole, this will be discussed in the final chapter.

The more we strip away the control mechanisms that have been placed upon us the more we seem to open up and discover our 'true self'.

'Over thinking' situations is a condition that has been placed on you, if you have any kind of problem in the circus of life then naturally as expected, we would seek the solution using thought. However over thinking a situation will almost never lead to a positive outcome. How many times during a situation that requires an answer that you've dwelled upon and found no solution, have you chosen to just sit down and try to clear your mind and not think at all, knowing that the answer will then come? Probably never knowingly, however some of the greatest solutions we have, often come at the point of no thought at all. All of a sudden the answer seems to appear from nowhere. You've held the problem at the forefront of your mind all day, then during your first quiet relaxing moment, it all begins to unfold clearly in your mind and the answer reveals itself to you.

Or for example, have you ever sat somewhere in silence and in the back of your mind you're holding a particular piece of information and then you watch, read or source some other non-related information that when it goes into your mind, dots join the two separate pieces of information, giving you a particular understanding that no one has seen, or different from what you were taught? These moments make total sense and resonate with a truth that cannot be questioned. We can call these moments epiphanies or 'eureka' moments. And if you've had one of these moments you cannot wait to get out there and tell someone, and then full of excitement you try to explain and most times they look at you like your strange? Or hopefully sometimes you explain it in a way that they understand it also. This is knowledge, inner insight, you understand it yet it hasn't been taught conventionally, the information has been connected and truth revealed by your own self, and the truth revealed from within.

I do hope not to confuse you, it does sound contrary when one moment I'm saying we should lose our limitations and think creatively and then in the next instance I'm saying do not think too much. I will try to explain the importance of actually needing both at times in your life.

It is essential to think and to be creative, by questioning we naturally find answers to seek. It is these answers to questions never asked before that can't be answered by just thought alone. Some will if not most, but some answers will remain elusive. At times of utter silence and with an empty mind the answers we seek become revealed from within, these are answers revealed from a source of power that connects all, the Universal consciousness.

As said previously this will be discussed in depth later on, I do fully understand how strange all this sounds, but please stay with me.

Whatever it is we do, once we stop just accepting things as are, and rather try and understand them better, and this is in regards to our whole life, then we slowly begin to become unconditioned from the grasp of social conditioning, and slowly our 'true selves', begin to be revealed.

We need to remind ourselves at times that we are pack animals, and naturally as humans we want to fit in because fitting in is a safe way to exist. However, humans sadly do not exist anymore as pack animals as we compete, we act outside of natural human behaviour because of money, a substance that separates and divides man. So naturally the pack conditioned mindset no longer suits what modern day society requires. More than ever we need to be different, to supply something different to consumers, or the world in whatever form we choose, because being different and great at what we do will yield great rewards. Alternatively, be part of the pack, working long hours for a minimum wage, a lifestyle that will take you to your grave quicker and poorer.

We also need to understand that the pack mentality, the copying to fit in, the mirroring of others to be liked and accepted can be our greatest weakness, as this means in essence we are being led.

I find it strange that as a pack animal creature we have in essence lost our way in that we do not fully as a whole, look after all of the pack. And yet in contrast the part of being a pack animal that is damaging, the copying of one another due to the wish to be accepted because of the fear of being rejected, we hold on to.

If the world was a happy place, that was as a 'whole' safe, and all the people had regular meals and access to medicine, then being led wouldn't be so bad, but we're being led the wrong way. Money is still the main concern, money over children's welfare, money over health and money over the welfare of the planet that we live on. A planet so special it supports a beautiful variety of life within the Animal Kingdom. And still we look in the vast cosmos of space for a planet like our own, because of how rare our home is. And still we destroy it.

Then there is war. I'm not naive, I do understand that sometimes a nation has no choice but to defend itself. But how many wars have we took part in when there hasn't been any threat? And only the threat the media tells us about? War for money, disregarding human life. War that has billions of pounds spent on it each year, billions of pounds that could be spent elsewhere, like medicine for the sick, food for the hungry as well as sourcing and implementing alternative energy sources less damaging to our planet. It could all be so very different.

So, what significance does this have on your life? It has a massive effect on your life; look at the world around you and look at the average person within your society, is that what you want? Or would you like more? Would you like to do the job that makes you happy? Do you want to fulfil a lifelong passion or dream? Would you like a better more fulfilling, loving and productive existence? Would you like more family time? Well you can have all this and be financially successful. The first step toward doing this is to step away from the pack mentality and to start listening to that still and almost silent voice within, the one that sings a different tune to the rest.

I heard the following quote one morning whilst listening to a motivational video in the shower. The moment I heard it, it rang with so much truth and seemed so appropriate to what I felt inside. Here it is...

2. *'If a man doesn't keep pace with his companions, perhaps he's listening to the beat of a different drummer. Let him dance to the music that he hears no matter how measured or far apart'.*

Henry David Thoreau.

Being different is a blessing, it truly is. Only creative thinkers can do something new and never seen before or produce something never heard before. However, a lot of creative souls will struggle in life because of not fitting in. They battle to be the same as everyone else, rather than accept their 'true self'. So many bright flames have been extinguished because of the struggle of life. Embrace your uniqueness, and accept that you are different then use it to its fullest potential and you will succeed.

If you step back and look at what you are taught, and how we are conditioned unknowingly by even our own loving family as children then all we have become is a unique cultural library of information, ancestral information and social political information.

So, who are you? Who is the real you? Are you truly content? Have you found your true purpose? Do you even know what your true purpose in life is? Do you consciously contribute positively to the world?

Let us consider this being your last day on this planet, and you have no choice but to have to go to work. If you somehow had the insight and knew that you were going to die this same evening, would you be happy doing what you would normally do on this day? If the answer is yes then you are clearly pursuing your life's dream, life's calling, your soul mission or whatever you want to call it.

But if the answer is no then you seriously need to take a step back and begin to question who you are? And what your true purpose is? Or if this all sounds too much then do what the majority of society does and kick back, relax and walk around with eyes wide shut hoping tomorrow will be different.

Life is short, and no one ever gets a second chance. You are here today and literally gone today in the big story of life. We should all know this, we've all lost in life yet we forget these simple truths every day, when we open our eyes and subject our soul to another day of the grind. Pursuing materialistic gains that serve no nourishment or nurture to our 'true self', doing something that by our own admittance if it was our last day, we wouldn't do it. So therefore, what is the point in doing this to begin with? Why live lives, day in day out that we don't want to live?

A big part of social conditioning contains fear, our design by nature is to have fear, being fearful can keep you alive, but we must be careful when we're conditioned as a pack. In time, we can become fearful of thinking a different view from the pack. We must remain true to ourselves and not merely do or believe certain viewpoints just because our friends or family have that viewpoint.

Think about how many times you may have argued a strong point, maybe an argument about politics or religion, and spoke with such conviction. My question to you is how much do you follow politics then? Do you truly listen to all political parties or do you simply vote the way you do because your parents share that view, or your friends? Or maybe your vote is swayed by the particular class that you are from within society.

To gain a true viewpoint to argue you would need to truly understand all possible options. Merely voting a certain way because of an ingrained handed down belief is wrong.

I hear such strong arguments in my line of work regarding religion as well. Unfortunately, with recent events around the world Muslim people globally have, and are still facing a lot of negative attention. When people come out with negative comments that are spoke with such strong belief I quickly ask them if they have any idea how many Muslims there are around the world, and that these few numbers that parade themselves under the banner of Islam are not true Muslims at all. I also ask if they've studied Islam or studied the Quran. How can you comment on a section of people that you have very little understanding about? I would defend any individual that was innocent and do the same for anyone from any religion, any political party, any creed and any sexuality, the truth is the truth and should never be denied. You should never follow or believe purely based on what you are either conditioned by the media to believe, or just because the people you love believe a certain thing.

    A lot of problems would quickly disappear in the world if people were to step out of the fear mindset and pack mentality and cross the alien territory of unfamiliar culture and beliefs, and to investigate with eyes enriched by truth; the truth of no prior understanding, but a truth of discovering our own opinion. From our own investigation and own research into a particular subject.

    Unfortunately, because of our inherent human behaviour and pack mentality, this separation of the people by fear of those that are not in their pack is an easy tactic to execute. And the fear of not being accepted by the pack helps keeps the majority belief alive. Once the majority accept a particular viewpoint then the rest of the group will quickly follow, if not we think we will be rejected. We're conditioned mentally to fear anything that maybe different from our own particular pack. People of different religions, different races, all these fears put in place by the powers that be to separate and to control you.

    The separation of society is encouraged by the powers that be and it is an old tactic that can be easily executed. The reasons are simple; to divide and conquer. You divide a nation, not just once but several times, by race, religion, social background, cultural differences, and many more, depending on what the individuals in that society attach their identity to. Once divided it becomes much easier to control a society, there is no need for conquering when you can condition and control a nation by executing simple techniques of division. These techniques are used as tactics by the powers that be to simply divide you from your fellow man, and control you. Boxes to put you in where you can sit uncomfortably picking fault with anyone from a different group of society, all the time missing the obvious truth, if we weren't busy fighting we would naturally as a people begin to truly integrate. And see the truth rather than be told the truth, and ultimately free our minds.

      A big part of our society becomes controlled by fear that even the fear of failing at anything makes them become rigid. Making them accept what is safe and stable, to never step out of their comfort zone. And in some cases people can even develop the fear of becoming successful and then not being able to handle the pressures this may bring to their already over complicated life. Fear, fear, fear!

      Living in this way does nothing to enrich you, it actually slowly destroys you, holds you back, and slowly the dreams and the ideas that were uniquely given to you by the Universe begin to disappear through the course of your life. We listen to what our parents say, partners and peers and slowly the voice inside that knows our true purpose, that once screamed out loud your passion, becomes quieter and quieter and slowly we begin to believe and accept that we didn't deserve our dream to be a reality. Then over time we develop the mentality to 'just get by', and most times short change our true potential and ultimately, we settle for less. We console ourselves with accepting that most people don't go on to live their dreams, we consciously accept that this must be reality. But of course, it isn't, reality is what we choose our reality to be as discussed in the introduction. So, do not allow yourself to get off this way, I hear people say things like "My life's not that bad, look at poverty, look at the homeless, my life is ok", or "This is the real world, I do what I have to do to get by to feed my family." These are cop outs, nothing more than weak minded answers for closed minded people that are happy to settle for much less than what had been intended for them.

    Of course, we have to support our families, my point is by discovering your true purpose you will end up with more money than you already have to support them, with the addition of more free time and a life free from stress where you are not simply worked into the ground by the toils of life. And unfortunately, we have been conditioned to think this way by our teachers, parents and anybody we have chosen to sit and listen to. I'm not saying listening and learning from our parents is wrong, as in most cases our parents love us dearly, however we must remember that our parents were conditioned and so were their parents the generation before them. By society, education and all other methods of conditioning.

    What about the people that do not choose to live this conditioned way? They are the people that society looks up to. The stars, the athletes, the musicians, the leaders of people, the pioneers... in essence they are the greats!

    People are taught early to be afraid, to be afraid of making a fool of themselves, afraid to step away from the pack and march to the unique tune that comes from within themselves. Many listen to other people's opinions regarding their own dreams and actually take their opinion on board, even though it is not their dream and even though it was not created by them, people still choose to listen to that opposing person's opinion. You must trust your gut instinct and follow your heart. It seems to be true that our 'true self' already knows what we truly want to become.

If you have a dream or talent or ambition then it came into existence when you did, it was born with you. It wasn't given to anyone else, that's why when you talk to people about it they don't understand it like you do, so why do you listen to them? Primarily because as mentioned time and time again we are pack animals, because we have been conditioned to believe that we are not strong enough to take on these challenges ourselves. So, rather than find the answer within, we seek salvation from our friends and family, because it is here we feel safe, just slowly treading shallow water all the time avoiding the deep end. Sadly, just getting by is a destroyer of dreams, yet ultimately, we think it is safe here. And what does living this way do towards our own souls being enriched and discovering our own true purpose? It does nothing.

Our society conditions us to work towards purchasing more, and ultimately owning more. More means we're successful out there in the crazy materialistic world, but truthfully more means absolutely nothing, just objects given value by a system it serves, objects you leave behind when your time comes to leave here. The point I'm trying to make is that you should not measure your life's worth on what you have accumulated in your bank account, this is the materialistic thought pattern that will hold you subservient to a system that wants more and more of your money, making you work more and more and in essence lose sight of the truly important things in life like family, children or pursuing your dream. So instead you should rather measure your life's worth on the true treasures of the Universe, which are, the 'realisation of self' and its importance, good intention, love, family, integrity in one's self, and truth. Truth to yourself and truth to the world around you, and discovering your purpose. Do we need reminding that when we die we take none of it with us? From the moment you begin to walk down the path of money and material goods as a solution to the soul's inner desire you begin a distracted existence that will put out your loved ones, blur your true desires and worst of all most probably work you straight into an early grave.

    There is a large portion of society doing jobs that they don't want to do, living lives they hate, in relationships that make them unhappy, going to work and grafting daily for just enough to get by, working for someone else, in fact working to help fulfil someone else's dream, and it is as simple as that. If you don't work toward your life's dream then you will work for somebody else's dream, it really is that simple. Why shouldn't you begin to live life on your terms? Live a life that is beneficial to yourself and your family. We are meant to be free yet we act as if we were enslaved when given the freedom to create our own reality. The only place I'm aware of that restricts your freedom is a prison, so if you are not in prison you have the freedom to do what you wish. Once we begin to adopt a fearless and free attitude towards our own life, it becomes possible to truly do what we wish to do, which is pursue our own purpose.

    If it is money you seek and let's be honest we do need money to make our family secure and hopefully secure the future of our family, then beginning to pursue your own purpose will bring more money than you ever thought. It will come with ease, but to simply chase money as a goal in life will ultimately be your biggest distraction to what your true calling is. A massive amount of people believe having money means you are successful, however it is the opposite of what is true. You cannot have money without first being successful.

Our uniqueness is our greatest gift. Whatever your inner calling is, no one can do it the way you can do it. By pursuing your purpose, and nurturing it, even failing at times and learning from these failings, by putting everything we have into it, we then begin a path towards mastery, and with mastery comes a price. Mastery comes with a high price in modern society and a price that will enable us to not just get by, but to live more comfortable, to have better holidays, to buy property for our future generations of family. Surely this is better than working all hours for someone else, going home tired every day to a family you wish you could give more time and more security to. Working your body into an early grave for somebody else, all the time watching your boss drive the flash car whilst hearing the whispers among fellow colleagues of where the boss has been this month on holiday. Do you see the point I'm trying to make? If you are going to work so hard every day like so many do, then why not do it for yourself? Your boss does, so why not you?

The first step toward discovering who you truly are, away from the conditioned self is to let go of fear and see fear for what it is. Fear is thought induced, it manifests from within our own mind. Winston Churchill puts it simply,

3. *"We have nothing to fear but fear itself"*.

And this is so true, fear will take years off your life, literally age you, destroy you, make you hide away and lose the valuable and short time you were given here. Fear is a killer, rather than just 'being' and enjoying life, you become that fearful you never even try those things that you know you're capable of doing because fear holds you back, and can through a fear projected mentality make you never get to pursue your life purpose, and be your 'true self'.

Your realisation of your 'true self' is of grand importance. It is key here for me to say that these thought patterns geared toward the freedom of your 'true self' should not serve as an excuse to go out and simply do what you want regardless of the consequence of others. Your true calling will benefit others and the world around you in a way that is far too complex to even try to understand. Take a look at the intricacy of nature and how one system supporting its goals will be connected somehow to another biological system which benefits from it. Does the honey bee realise its own importance? No, it simply lives out its chores. Your true calling and manifestation of your own reality through acceptance of the importance of 'self' is of a great importance. As we said in the introduction, like God, or the 'Universal consciousness', we too are creators of our reality. This is so important. As we create we change the world ourselves, and create a new world, it's a partnership between us and God. As we create and make things better, so does God's creation evolve and become better. There is a partnership at work here, a partnership between the Universe and everything within it. Can you see the significance now of your own existence? The importance of who you are and the significance of the 'realisation of self'?

We as a species have become disattached from the importance of 'self' and thus lost the balance between ourselves and the world around us. Just look at what living the way we do as done to our planet? Can we think of any other creature on Earth that does this? That destroys its own habitat?

When I say the 'realisation of self' what I mean is the realisation of the importance of self. There are billions of self-centred people on this planet, and this is not what I mean by the 'realisation of self', unfortunately few realise their true potential and what effect their life has on the world around them. The 'realisation of self' is about realising your own significant part in the construction of your own reality but also your effect on the immediate world around you. It is a law like any other scientific physical law.

Your actions have an effect. It is the law of consciousness, the manifestation of the world around us by our thoughts and actions. Like any law in physics you cannot operate outside of it, you are and have always been a part of it. And like any law of physics you get results based on what you initially put in. There is no bad luck, no victims, no punishment by an almighty God that unfortunately religion has made to be the image of man, a God that is angry unless pleased with prayer and practised doctrines. This is not true, the consciousness of the Universe does not punish, you simply receive the results of the fruits of your creation of reality. If you are positive then you receive a positive outcome, if negative naturally a negative outcome. No one ever baked a tasty cake from poor ingredients, think about it.

The world is full of people that tried to gain in life by misleading others, people that have tried to gain at the expense or hurt of others, or people that chose a path of wanting to do nothing. You will find these people worldwide in prisons or sleeping rough somewhere with no fixed abode. Some will actually financially succeed for a while, but eventually, in one way or another karma will deal its hand. You can't cheat life!

So back to what we were discussing, can we think of any other species that willingly destroys its own habitat for personal gain? No, and why is this? Somewhere along the way a big part of society has developed an attitude to point the finger elsewhere. All the time avoiding the plain truth; it is our personal responsibility to make the changes needed to save this beautiful planet. We will look anywhere for blame rather than place the emphasis on ourselves. The plain truth is simple, it's us right now that chooses to do nothing to save our Earth, our conditioned minds have been busied by the pursuit of more and we have forgotten how to listen, how to listen to our own direction and purpose, and instead we develop a personality that can never be coined 'human nature'. How can our behaviour be called human nature when we're driven toward a substance that has no relevance toward the Earth or the Universe as a whole, and that substance is money? If you're thinking this isn't true, then please just stay with me here.

There are a lot of global businesses in various fields and even politicians that have clearly shown at various times a lack of concern for the environment or for people in their own pursuit of greater profit margins with their own pockets being lined by corporations, this unfortunately has always gone on. Then there are sports goods manufacturers sourcing cheaper labour in countries with poor laws to protect the working man or child, leaving them vulnerable to working extremely long hours for very little pay. There are also oil companies destroying eco systems globally, putting the emphasis on profit rather than on the world around them. Each generation leaving the problem for the next generation that follows.

We have seen in this chapter how we have been

conditioned through the media to buy certain products and how we are brainwashed into dogmatic thinking. And we have seen how the system serves the few rather than the many, and as we know the system is all based around money. Money drives everything and it is the men behind the money that rule and control everything. Money quite simply is power. How many of us were encouraged to borrow and spend during the 90's and then lost a fortune when the economy collapsed recently here in the U.K? How many people are still paying off debt or in fact will never be debt free? How many people currently live month to month having to use high street loan companies that again charge massive amounts of interest that force certain folk into a system of struggle?

  This corporate driven media brainwashing is not just limited to current fashions, trends etc. These huge companies play a role in the system, to that there is no doubt. But there are other systems in place, that ensure global companies from different backgrounds also dictate to a certain extent the way you live.

  The pharmaceutical companies need a long hard look at; a system where a pill for one ailment will in years to come most probably lead you to taking a pill for another ailment. Medicine is of paramount importance, there is no doubt. However, there are a lot of conditions where more safer alternatives could be used, safer methods with no medicines, just education to the patient based on a new outlook towards life, with a better diet and a healthier lifestyle. It is interesting to note that Hippocrates the Father of modern day medicine way back in 431 B.C said that the key to being healthy was to,

4. *'Let thy food be thy medicine'.*

How many times have you sat with your G.P and

discussed making changes to your diet based on your own health problems? I don't mean a discussion where the doctor simply tells you to go on a diet because you are overweight. I mean specific discussions to resolve key problems.

For example, depression is a major issue in modern day living. Did you know Niacin a natural vitamin also known as Vitamin B3 has been scientifically proven to lower depression levels? Niacin has been medically proven to help against heart disease, child diabetes, cancer, depression, schizophrenia and even in studies helped alcoholics in recovery (please feel free to take a look online, there are many papers available on this). And yet it is the last thing a Doctor will tell you to go and take if you were to walk into the surgery on a Monday morning feeling down. Niacin is just one essential vitamin that the body needs. There are several essential vitamins that provide the human body with everything it needs to stay healthy and to repair itself.

It has also been discovered that a 30-minute walk 5 times a week has been proven scientifically to help lose weight, lower blood pressure, reduce diabetes and lower stress levels. There are huge amounts of data supporting these findings. With modern day living, how many people actually think that they have the time to walk 30 minutes a day for 5 days a week? Most people will be under the illusion that they simply do not have the time, as life is too busy. Yet these same people will happily watch several episodes of T.V. one after another on any given evening.

Another huge life distraction is the economy and how we allow the big powers of the world, the banks and multitrillion dollar corporations to manipulate societies living conditions by setting us up to fall. We've already spoke about how we are conditioned by society to chase money, the elusive paper gold, this is what makes money powerful. It should be no shock then that the people with the most money hold the most power. These are not the leaders of nations. Take time and look at some of the information available regarding world debt. 99% of the world is in debt. Country after country. Here in the United Kingdom the debt as a nation has reached the trillions. This is the same as the U.S.A. An apparent super power yet massively in debt. Russia and China are also the same. As are most countries, however most nations seem to have debt in the billion-dollar range, and some in the million-dollar range. Only here and in the U.S is the debt so high. So, who are the people behind the companies that these governments owe money to?

These people are the most powerful players on the global stage, they are the Elite. This small percentage of the population (around 2%) own nearly all the global money. These families are mainly centred around the banking system. However, these families also own or have controlling shares in the world's leading pharmaceutical companies, oil companies and tons of multinational companies. This type of global monopoly comes under the guise of many different company names and allows the Elite to manipulate the global stock markets with ease. Creating a recession is easy when there is this type of control being executed.

I remember the last recession this country had, it was around 2008-9. I can clearly remember Gordon Brown, the British Prime Minister at the time stating that the country was heading into a recession, not that the country WAS in a recession, but that it was heading into one. And so, what did most of the British public do? They panicked and stopped spending as much (worst case scenario for any economy). Which slowed the economy down and took us head first into a recession!!

It is these Elite powers that now own countries, by indebting them. The same way we as a people were encouraged to spend when the economy was good. Spending and borrowing beyond our means, then wham!! The economy collapsed, wages got lowered and now some of the people cannot afford to make the previously agreed financial arrangements. Meaning the bank calls in the debt another way, usually selling the property you live in. The property you were encouraged to buy, the property all your money has gone into. So, for example you buy a property for £200,000 and pay the initial 20% deposit of £40,000 that you have saved the last few years for. This means the bank has borrowed you the rest which is £160,000 plus any interest charges. After making repayments for the next 10 years you manage to pay back a further £60,000. At this point let us say the economy crashes and house prices fall. Your lovely £200,000 home has now depreciated massively to just £140,000. You go to work and discover you've been given less hours or maybe had a pay cut or even been made redundant due to the economy crashing. So now payments to the bank cannot be made. What does the bank do? After several months of missing payments, the bank does what it can to return its own investment. Remember the bank borrowed you £160,000 of which you paid £60,000 back. So naturally you now own the bank £100,000 plus any interest. This means that your house purchased for £200,000 has now been sold for £140,000 (due to the recession). Once the bank has taken back what it is owed plus interest charges and solicitors fees and estate agents etc. have been paid, it will be no surprise to discover that not only are you homeless but you are also out of pocket. Out of pocket for the initial £40,000 deposit and £60,000 paid back in repayments. Homeless and down £60,000. Where is the £60,000? It is in the bank...not your bank though!

    This system is no accident, it is a business. A system that watches and monitors you. A system that has ripped families apart, seen suicide rates increase when the economy falls, yet a system happy to keep making you chase the things just beyond your material reach. A system happy to condition you from birth to seek money, as the system makes profit after more profit. A system clearly happy to then manipulate your material conditioning to set you up to fail, purely to take more from you.

    So, we have been conditioned. Conditioned for a purpose, a purpose that builds our material possessions whilst all the time filling the pockets of corporations with more cash. Even at the cost it seems on occasions, of ourselves and our own planet. So, what is the alternative? The alternative is becoming free from this mindset and discovering who your unconditioned self is, your 'true self'. The person you were designed to be, not just a generic clone of society but a child of this Universe.

    Everything in the Universe has a purpose, from the trees that produce the oxygen we breathe, to the bees that gather nectar from the flowers that in turn cross pollinate and further aid the flowers future survival, to the Sun in the sky that brings life to our world and the surrounding solar system, everything it seems serves a purpose in this life. And yet most seem to not know their own unique purpose. We now know why, and it is through conditioning. You've been conditioned to believe your purpose is to simply exist and gain materialistic belongings, nothing more.

    So, the answer it seems in the quest of discovering your 'true self' is to become unconditioned. To become totally free of society and its dogmatic thinking, you need to let go of two of your oldest friends. Two friendships developed over your lifetime, ego and fear.

Chapter 3

Releasing Ego And Fear. Discovering The 'True Self'.

Now you know a little bit of the truth regarding the system and what the system has done to condition you to serve itself.

So with this in mind do you want to continue living a life based on their terms? Now you can see what role the Elite powers want you to play, why play it? Why sit like a subservient dog behaving just how you have been conditioned to? Why not step up and play this 'game of life' on your terms? Why not discover your own purpose and pursue it? Why be a spectator playing the safe conditioned systematic game?

In fact, we have seen with the recession and other factors, that the 'safe' option is in fact not safe at all. Life is still going to drop you to your knees at some point, one day as you go to your job that you hate but do so just to get along. The phone will ring and the messenger of misery will be there to shake you to your knees like a child, and that, as we all eventually learn when we sit and think about it, is life. We have upon us as humans, elements with which we have to learn to control and to learn disattachment to, these are fear and ego respectively. Fear will keep you living the illusion of the 'safe' option and your ego will convince you that it is the right way to live.

You can't release ego until fear is eradicated from your day to day thinking. Ego is constructed from fear, as ego is a projected falsified self, constructed from within to mask and cloak parts of ourselves we may deem inadequate compared to our fellow man. So, ego is a projected better version, or that's what we believe.

    Fear is a condition put on ourselves either by our self or from an external factor, i.e. an outward source, someone's words that somehow encourage the fear trail of thought. Ultimately though it is only ourselves that can conquer it, and conquering our own fears will bring about the true treasures and rewards of life. We spend our life trying to avoid pain trying to avoid hurt, trying to avoid failure yet it is in these moments that something magical happens to our own being, soul or consciousness. Those who have shown no fear and yet have been knocked down and had the strength to get up, always get up stronger and more educated so that whatever put them down to begin with won't find it so easy the next time, and this is the magic; our pain, our hurt, our hurdles, all define us, all mould and shape us into a stronger version than the previous one, all the while reshaping our consciousness. Therefore, embrace your pain, embrace your failures, accept that failing and pain are just factors in this game called life, and that the challenges of life fall on all, life is simply life.

    There is not one single creature on this planet that doesn't have to battle every day for food, water or just plain survival. This is the nature of our Universe and sadly we forget this because of how easy we obtain the essential items of life from birth, like water, food and shelter. We are at the greatest point of man's own history regarding technology and the ease of life. Yet this ease of life has had the effect of making a big majority of the people 'soft' and 'weak'. To the point where we actually think life is hard...when in fact life has never been easier. An analogy would be the spoilt child. When did you ever see a spoilt child show gratitude? The spoilt child has so much given without ever truly needing anything that the child actually does not appreciate the biggest gestures.

Embrace the struggle, embrace the fear, see it for what it is. You will hear some people compare themselves to a lion, comparing their own strength to that of the fierce predator. And yet the lion will never face the fear of being afraid of a more ferocious predator, other than the challenge of another male maybe for dominance within the pack. Now consider the water buffalo, it isn't fearsome or ferocious, and yet this creature displays the courage of a samurai warrior. Why? Every time they go down to the local watering hole for a drink, several of the pack will never return and will be attacked from the water as they drink by crocodiles, literally. And yet despite this the water buffalo will return again when it needs water. Why? Because it has no choice, and it will do whatever it takes to survive....even risk its own existence! It is not just the lion that has strength, you will find it prevalent throughout all nature.

    I'm not saying that you should live in a way that invites trouble and unwanted challenges in to your life because that would be pretty thoughtless, however what I am saying is that you should no longer be afraid of taking on life because of fear. Fear should never be the dominant force in holding anyone back from pursuing their life goals. The times in life that truly knock us off our feet always come when we don't expect them to, and these sad, heart-breaking moments usually have nothing to do with any of our own actions. Therefore, living in fear serves you no purpose, all it does is slowly destroy you and permanently take you away from living your own life purpose.

    So, what is fear? Is fear a solid entity we can touch? No, of course not. Fear is a manifestation from within ourselves; what one man is fearful of, another man may laugh at, so is there any truth within fear? It seems not, as no fear is a universal fear.

Now danger is different, I'm not saying be fearful of nothing ever again, because that would be pretty stupid. If your fear emanates from a clear sense of impending danger, then please listen to what your mind is telling you and get to a safe position. However, I'm talking about self-induced fear, fear over nothing. For example, the singer that is full of talent but never makes it to the audition because of the fear of failing, or the fear of not performing to their best level. How about those that fear death? Death is waiting for us all and should serve as a reminder to how precious life is. So, embrace it.

Think about this, fear is not a solid entity that can actually harm you, but rather a manifestation from your own mindset, how many times have you been fearful of something happening that never actually played out? I bet there are countless times throughout your childhood and into your adult life that you've rested your head on your pillow at night and worried yourself endlessly about something that has never actually happened. So why live in fear? It is much more fulfilling to live with the world around you accepting that challenges are there to be relished, and that there is nothing to fear, but instead everything to gain.

Once you begin to accept life this way, standing tall and relishing the challenges, then the horizon of life becomes a lot clearer; no more dogmatic mindsets that take us away from the fight, but rather a new horizon that relishes the challenge of life, relishes the thought of a battle with oneself to make the changes needed, and if life knocks you down then that is fine, because I've been down, weathered the storm and got back up. We all have our trials. Life trials are similar for all, it is how we handle these trials that separates us. Anyone that reads this and currently believes that failing and falling down makes you a failure is so very wrong. It doesn't matter if you try in life and lose, because from the loss you will gain so much experience that the next battle will be much easier, and after countless battles inevitably the time will come when the battle is actually won. When you were a child you did not stop trying to walk the first time you fell and hurt yourself. In fact, no doubt you probably fell many times trying to develop your walking legs as a child, not once did you ever think after you fell, 'I'm not trying that again'. Nature clearly designed us to keep trying. It is how we evolve, it is how the Universe evolves.

This is not failing this is learning and it is those that choose to not try that truly fail, those that are that scared of failing that they will not even attempt, but rather step back consoling themselves that they couldn't do it anyway, that is the failure and unfortunately the majority of the population live this way when it comes to what would be life changing decisions. Instead most stay safe and within their own particular comfort zone and choose fear rather than life.

It is not just important to release fear for yourself but for the world around you also, and hopefully in doing so you will free the minds of future generations. The point I'm making is simple, take a good look around you, look at the world you live in, look at what living this way leads to, humanity as a whole is being guided by corporations and banks, corporations and banks that want nothing more than more money regardless of the outcome to humanity or the world around them. Everything being orchestrated through fear and ego (we will discuss ego shortly). It doesn't take a genius to work out that man is on a collision course with wiping himself out via his own actions, always consumed by the notion of getting more, more, more, whilst all the time walking by and ignoring the state of society and our global ecosystem. We're killing ourselves and hurting the balance of our own planet and yet the masses seem uninterested and seem content knowing that it will be problems for future generations and not our own, because they are all so busy acquiring more. Another cop out, rather than us standing up and making the changes ourselves we just carry on about our own business, a society where people will quite happily walk past a person being attacked because they are scared of any repercussions that they might face if they were to say or do anything.

What has happened? Are we that locked and conditioned in a fear driven mindset that we would knowingly walk by a person that needs our help because of the fear of repercussions we might face ourselves? This is all wrong and we all know this deep inside. Thankfully it's not all doom and gloom, there are some that will do more, there are a small minority that will defend for the greater good, that will protect their fellow man. These people walk amongst us every day, the only difference is these people will not allow fear to control them, and instead these people change an incredibly negative situation into a positive situation that best exemplifies the good found within parts of humanity. A wise man named Mahatma Gandhi once said,

[5.] *'Be the change you wish to see in the world'.*

And it is as straight forward and as simple as that. Why should we look elsewhere for help? This is what social conditioning has led many to believe; a belief that we look elsewhere for change, look elsewhere for help, like who we vote for or even going to the local church and praying for help. When all the time the biggest truth has been taken from us, and that is that it is us as individuals that truly have the power to self-lead and help ourselves.

We are all born equal, and that is with a free mind. It is our own individual social environment that strips this freedom from us. A conditioning that imposes fear and a belief that we somehow get by with what we've got and that we don't deserve more. It is true that you will only get in life what you believe you deserve in life, so believe that you deserve more and be the creator you know you are.

Like I said at the very beginning of this book, we are all it seems God in miniature. We all create continuously. If we choose to live in fear, then we are creating a world from a fear induced false ego projection. Imagine how different the world would be if we began to live without fear and therefore created a new more positive reality? Just for a second let us take a little time out and do a short exercise. Close your eyes and picture the person you would like to be, the highest self of you, your divine self, one that is not scared of trying something new, one that's not judging a race of people based on a few but instead gives people a chance based on an individual level, the you that lives day to day consciously aware and always trying to become a better person. Now hold that projection in your mind and think how you would walk, talk and behave differently to the challenges life places upon you. Do you see a difference between that projection and the person you currently are? Most reading this probably will see a huge difference. By changing our actions, we naturally change our outcomes. The simple law of 'cause and effect'.

Just for a moment take a few seconds to think about the things you have allowed into your mind, the movies, music, conversations, the T.V. shows, the newspapers, magazines, journals etc. Just think about how all these things have altered your own mindset, how the media machine as well as your peers and your education have altered your own unique way of thinking. There is no point in denying it, we are all products of what we have seen, heard and spoke. Basically, I refer to this mass of information as 'content' and it is our very own 'content' that helps shape our ego and essentially becomes our character and ultimately our consciousness. If we view the content of our own consciousness as a material substance, then surely if we can somehow erase the content that is negative or change it then we can consequently change our own consciousness as a result. Or simply put, if we can destroy the ego we become our 'true self'. You may be reading this thinking, "Why is this important?"

  To strip oneself of as much conditioned media fed content as possible will slowly reveal your 'true self' again, the self that was born into the Universe full of ideas, eager to live life to the fullest, the spirit that was not tainted by someone else's thought patterns and beliefs. Your 'true self' that was put here with a purpose, a purpose that has most likely been forgotten, and in most instances never realised at all. I will touch on this in the final part of the book however before you reach those chapters here is a question; how many times have you heard someone say or even say yourself the words, 'I feel like there is something I'm meant to do in life' or 'I feel like there's something more for me' or as we spoke earlier 'what is my purpose?'

  If you are confused, then maybe you have seen a wonderful image that has travelled around social media for the past couple of years. The image is simple and it is of a white baby sitting next to a black baby, and both are smiling looking into each other's eyes holding hands with the caption, 'Nobody is born racist'. Does this not say it all about how dumb our conditioning can be? This image best expresses how destructive and wrongly developed our ego can become over time with an influence of negative conditioning.

What is the 'true self'? Well I can tell you point blank that you are not your 'true self'. You may be getting unsettled right now but that is your ego having a rage. Let us take a quick look at society as a whole and question are there any individuals? There are not many, because as humans we imitate others, rather than express ourselves from within. Many will choose to copy a role model that they admire, from wearing a certain style of clothing, to having a particular haircut, to eating certain diets because of celebrity culture, or worse having a personal involvement with a group mindset situation, i.e. racist groups, religious cults, even mainstream religion. All of these place you inside a box of imitation, and each one gives us profound examples of how damaging ego can be. Racism, quite simply one of the most ignorant conditions anyone could ever have, has been witness to terrible and brutal crimes throughout history because of someone else's colour and a twisted ego and mindset. And religion, an institution that should offer a safe place of belief in a creator with a love and compassion for others, can become so twisted and so dangerous that some followers of religion negate any other religion based on their own egotistical view of what they have been told. In the worst case, there have been murders in the name of religion. All the while ego taking them to a position of committing murder, a sin in itself but to also murder a fellow believer of God... ego is truly an insane device, and losing it will set you free.

Religion, despite its own good intentions can cause massive separation within communities as does racism. Here is a very interesting scientific truth for any racist; all people on Earth can be genetically traced back to Mitochondrial Eve, a lady that lived 144,000 years ago, in Africa. This it seems is true as my own family had their DNA tested and sure enough both my Nan and Grandad's genes both contain the gene linked to Mitochondrial Eve, and I'm on paper given the label 'white' and so are all my family. I find it particularly funny when I come into contact with white racists, because the white race has to be the most mixed race of all. I'm white so I have no problem saying this. We come in a wonderful array of variations, white people have blue eyes, brown eyes and green eyes and when it comes to hair colour you can see the full spectrum of colours available to humans, there is black hair, dark brown hair, medium brown hair, light brown hair, dark blonde hair, strawberry blonde hair, blonde hair, light blonde hair and white hair. Also, do not forget that there is also skin tone, which varies from as near to white as skin can be right through to a dark skin tone, all falling under the social box of white. I think it is fair to say that we're probably genetically the most mixed race of all.

      This planet is old, and Homosapiens (us) have it seems been around for a long time. We are truly a single species that has learned civility and spread across the globe. For some reason, however when our ancestors left Africa and then spent thousands of years apart and evolved to fit into their separate living environments and conditions, they returned a different colour, speaking a different language and it seems somewhere forgot their history. And from forgetting their ancient past, years of deaths, slavery and racism have followed. All because as a species we have a short time based opinion of who we are. My own personal truth is that I'm not white.........I am human, and my brothers and sisters speak all languages and come in a divine array of colours.

Back to ego and my other example which is the dangerous ego found in some religious people. If you are from a religious background then please accept that the story of God has been told a lot of times in several cultures and in different ways and has helped and aided believers worldwide, so when you are attacking another religion you are effectively attacking God, that which you hold so dear. I know if you're a devoted Christian then right now you will be sitting thinking 'I know Jesus is the light and the only path to God', the Catholic, the Muslim and the Jehovah's witness will all have different beliefs regarding the 'true' way to God. You can't all be the one and only 'true' way. Logic clearly suggests that even though none of these religions can be the only way, they all do in fact show a way. A loaf of bread may be La Pain in France or Bröt in Germany but it is still a loaf of bread. Different names have no effect on what it is.

How can you express yourself truthfully when from an early age, you've been conditioned to copy what is popular? Or maybe led by a religious system that conditions YOU to do what THEY deem right. There are religious groups out there that become the literal backbone within that particular groups society. The society becomes that embedded by religion that any member within the group will become fearful of ever believing anything different. Most of the time being repeatedly conditioned to believe that 'hell awaits those that do not follow'. Such utter nonsense displayed endlessly, time and time again. A blind faith handed down, generation after generation. We will chat deeper about religion in later chapters.

Let's examine your parents. It should be no great shock now to discover that they are imitations too, so in essence we are the evolution and social beings that are the product of 'generation after generation' of copycats.

Surely now you must begin to see just how 'not yourself' you have truly become. And that goes for all of us.

Before we go on to the next chapter, I want you to consider this; we have spoken about how as a society we are conditioned from birth on a number of different levels, some positive some negative but we agree that in some form or another a conditioning has taken place, hopefully now it should be easy to accept that all that this conditioning has given you is a consciousness ultimately bound in fear. A conditioning that has made you look elsewhere for help, and made you a copycat of whatever version of humanity you have aspired to be, whilst all the time taking the power of your individual self away from you.

The big question is why is all this important? I think if you've read this far then you probably understand its importance. The importance of being true to oneself, and discovering your 'true self', is your only true path, for it is here you shall discover your true purpose. The real challenge of life is knowing who we truly are and mastering ourselves, not others ever, but always ourselves.

I do not conform to any set religion and never will as I have discussed in this chapter, as any set religion or set belief places myself in a category of a group mentality, however whether you call the life force of the Universe, Consciousness, God, Allah, Brahma, Prana, Nature or whatever name you give it, then I can say this next statement with true knowing, there is a higher force at work in this Universe, and it is behind all that is and intertwined within the fabric of everything.

Just look at how complex the Universe is and how beautiful it is, there are some 500 billion stars in our galaxy, and around 500 billion galaxies in our known Universe. It is in fact said that there are more stars in the known Universe than grains of sand on this planet. Wow!!

You probably have never heard that the Universe itself is alive, and that the Universe is pure consciousness. This will be discussed in a later chapter. And as we are of the Universe, when we clear our minds of these socially conditioned material ties that bind us like ego and fear then we begin to hear our true calling. If you ever felt out of place in your job, life etc. then it's because you were destined for more and your true self knows this. You are of the Universe, born of stardust, born of consciousness and born from the higher consciousness of the Universe in which we live. You are not material based and the Universe is bigger and way more complex than you have ever been taught or ever even imagined. This is all to be discussed so please don't switch off and think that I have entered the realms of science fiction!

This Universe is full of life and anyone who is closed minded enough to think that life could only evolve on one planet out of the trillions that are out there in the Universe is clearly conditioned, and conditioned in a way that they never see or understand the grandness of the intelligent design they are born out of and are clearly a part of. I've spoken with friends from a religious background that truly believe we are the only intelligent life in all of the known Universe. How unfortunate that a group with a so called strong belief in God, are so ego based that they never see the true grandeur and glory of God's work. Instead focusing their grandeur on man himself. It truly is a loss.

The truth is science was originally shaped by certain religious beliefs regarding our solar system, placing Earth at the centre of everything. Naturally as science developed these original ideas became replaced with science facts. And science fact is that Earth is not the centre of everything at all and in actuality we are about as significant as a bubble in the ocean. Early belief made the assumption that there was no life out there in the cosmos which became further strengthened after we failed to discover any intelligently evolved life within our own little town called the Solar system. So the early scientists made this assumption based on the very few facts they had at hand, however in this new age when we consider what we now know, and that is that the Universe seems to be infinite with an uncountable amount of stars and an uncountable amount of planets it must be fair to say that life has to be out there, in fact it shouldn't take any imagination to assume this, if we are here then quite frankly other life is out there too.

Let us consider the notion of there being nothing, no life out there at all in the known Universe. Firstly it would be a huge waste of space and we would have to be some sort of anomoly to the way things should be. We would have to be an accident. And the Universe tends to not have accidents. Secondly everywhere we look in the world around us we see life, and it is literally everywhere. Therefore if the Universe displays certain physical laws, then it makes total sense that whatever is going on here has to be happening in a similar fashion elsewhere.

Many scientists are coming forward now with this new thought pattern to the Universe and slowly the world is catching up. Only a few years ago the United Nations appointed an Ambassador to Earth, so if any contact was made we now have Earth's representative. Even the Catholic Church changed its belief on life elsewhere in our Universe to one that now includes the possibility of other life being out there.

So, the World is changing on this one belief

system, which should show you the reader how wrong a worldly belief can be. Is this not an example of social conditioning? Is this not an example of how wrong a society can be in their thinking? Is this an example of how truth itself can be a variable? Because a few hundred years ago, people believed that we were the centre of all things and that life could only exist here and nowhere else and at that time this was the 'truth', however a hundred years later or so we discovered that the Sun is at the centre of our solar system, and our Sun itself is travelling within its own galaxy 'the Milky Way' in which it revolves around a massive black hole. And that our galaxy the 'Milky Way' is just one of around 500 billion other galaxies. From these discoveries, we can see how man's beliefs, 'content' or consciousness has evolved, and with a greater understanding.

 Regarding life out there in the cosmos, we just don't know, however what we do know is that evidence suggests that life is in fact out there, in fact evidence would suggest that extra-terrestrial life has been interacting with this planet for a long time, but that's another discussion.

 Hopefully now it is easier to see how wrong it is to simply believe something just because the masses do, how easily it is to be taken down a path of thought that at the centre is wrong from the start. What is important from this is that it clearly shows that we should always question and not just accept facts as so, we do not need to be shown, to be taught, to be guided from external forces, but rather instead we need to give ourselves the captain's role, and lead and teach and master ourselves, continually growing on a path of 'self-discovery', 'self-truth' and 'self-nourishment', accepting nothing as just fact, but seeking the answer our self. This is our own unique path, this is learning and this is self-mastery. Once you open up and accept your own importance of self and take on the responsibility of creator within a partnership with God, then slowly the Universal consciousness and the secrets of everything will slowly over time be revealed.

There is no leader to follow, no false idol to worship, no saviour to ask for help, instead you are the leader, you are of the Universe and your worship goes inward as you realise that you are created of the Universe and you are special, and finally you are the saviour. Because as you may already know at most times in life it is only ourselves that can truly help ourselves.

If you have no belief in God or a higher force, then that is fine as we will discuss this in later chapters. A lot of people struggle with the belief of an omnipotent force, and sadly this has happened mainly and ironically because of religion itself, and social conditioning. The leading atheists love religion, as they can find it so easy to dissect the stories, and pull them apart as laughable.

Doing the job that I do means I meet a good cross section of society, and I will often out of interest ask a customer if they are a believer or not. Nearly all say no, and sadly say no with no reason as to why they do not believe. Most simply don't, so it seems easier for a large part of society to say no and just fit in with the masses. And yet a lot of my customers that have no belief often have religious tattoos. This really intrigues me. As this best exemplifies the bizarre effect of social conditioning, having a tattoo with no meaning personally in any way, yet marking the skin with such profound images purely for the aesthetic pleasure or simply 'what it looks like'. What is even more interesting and reflective of social conditioning, is the fact that these nonbelievers will only ever have Christian images. Again, reflecting their heritage and ancestral values. For a joke (I love to see people's reactions) I often ask customers why they don't want an image of Shiva, the Hindu God or maybe Muhammed? These nonbelievers all react the same.... not impressed!! I quickly remind them that Jesus had brown skin too, and also came from faraway lands in the Middle East. A lot of my customers look shocked when I say this as they have clearly never thought about it. I get the feeling at times that their impression of Jesus is of a white man with blue eyes.

So here basically we have a mindset that will have tattoos based on a subject that they have no belief of, yet still insist that they have the religious belief associated with their own heritage. This is social conditioning exemplified. It is mindless! All these material ties do is give out false projections of who you are. And who are you? You are the most powerful force in your Universe. This is no understatement. Just look scientifically at what we now know about ourselves. It is strange yet true that religions greatest opposition, science has done what religion has sometimes failed to do. That is to show with profound evidence the existence of intelligent design within our Universe, it now also shows us that everything is connected on a subatomic level. If you have no prior understanding of physics, then that is fine. Basically, subatomic particles are the smallest building blocks of life and construct everything around us, including us.

We will discuss the quantum realm or subatomic realm later in the book. Before we do I just want to bring something to light that you may or may not have heard or seen. There has been an attempt by some scientists to dumb down the connection between ourselves as humans and our connection to the subatomic realm. Certain scientists like to suggest that even though the quantum realm displays all sorts of strange and unusual properties (for instance the smallest particles that hold us together do not act within the realms of time and space, and display unusual properties of them all being connected and all the quantum particles of the Universe seem to be one whole being), that it has no connection to us. This thought pattern baffles me so I want you to think about this; if you were to build a house with bricks and then apply a coat of plaster rendering, is it still not made of bricks? Or are we to assume that it is just made of plaster? The truth as we know is that it is made of both. Just because we only see the rendered outside finish does not mean the bricks are not of significance. They clearly hold it all together. What I'm saying is that the smallest particles of ourselves naturally are part of us, and the magic that seems to be displayed within the smallest parts of ourselves is clearly a part of us too. And it is this part of us that answers so many questions that have puzzled man for such a long time.

Chapter 4

Separating The Creator From Religion, And Walking Forward.

Firstly, before we start this chapter can I just say again that I do not follow any particular religion, can I also state without any doubt that I firmly know God exists, although my thoughts are unimportant as regards to your own viewpoint.

I do want to put across to you the reader how strong my 'knowing' is. I use the term 'knowing' rather than 'believing' as I truly have no doubt regarding there being a creator to our Universe.

I know the world doubts the existence of a creator, let's be honest if we take the world's bestselling religious book the Bible, we can see that it does itself no favours, as its size, the time it was written and therefore its very understanding are far too hard to comprehend for most people today, however what it does say like most other religions within its text is that the Universe had a start or a creation point and this is of massive importance.

The Bible talks of a creator and so does the Quran, as well as other religions. Most of the biggest religions worldwide all clearly make the same point, and that point is that the Universe had a point of creation and naturally a creator. This may not seem that important to most, however it is important to note that some of these books are at their oldest around 3500 years old. The scientific belief was contrary to this until 1929, before 1929 the science community took the view that space was eternal, that it was inert and that it had been around forever and would remain forever. In 1929 the astronomer Edwin

Hubble came along and discovered with tests and analysis of his observations that the Universe in fact did have a creation point! And thus, the Big bang theory was put forward and is now readily accepted as the acceptable theory regarding the beginning of our Universe.

Does this mean these ancient books are right? Well regarding the beginning of our Universe, they seem to be bang on the mark, in fact so accurate it took science around 1900 years to catch up with what the Bible had said. The Hindu texts which are arguably some of the oldest texts on Earth also speak of a creator, although these books take the view further, the Hindu's believe that the Universe is cyclical in nature, and that this Universe is not the first and nor shall be the last to be created by Lord Brahma. Indicating that many universes have come before our own. Not only is this religion stating creation but it is also describing the end of the Universe, and with it the beginning of another.

Does this mean anything that religion had a creation point and yet science did not? Maybe, maybe not, but it's certainly food for thought. Here we see clear beliefs laid out in different texts that all point to a creation point, beliefs that were all contrary to science theory, until 1929 when science had to rewrite its text books regarding the history and beginning of our Universe. Personally, I find it profound that these ancient books had nailed the fact that our Universe did indeed have a start point.

Let's not make any mistakes I'm by no means trying to denounce any of the sciences. The point I want to make though is that science deals with facts. A scientific approach can never show any belief toward a creator so will endeavour to try and believe and prove that the Universe was 'spontaneously created' from nothingness. Rather than accept the logical truth which is that spontaneous creation does not happen. And if spontaneous creation does not exist then it logically only leaves one conclusion...'divine creation'.

Religion does cause a divide within society and within groups, and yet despite their own differences over the minor details it does seem evident that certain themes do occur throughout all religions. What I find interesting about religion is that most religions have a prophet, deity or a saviour, lets list some examples; there is Jesus Christ, Buddha, and Muhammed to name but a few. I'm not going to get into an argument over which one is the true way, but for the sake of this discussion let's consider that they maybe all are. Not the truth or way as regards to what they say, but the truth as regards to their actions.

We cannot and should not for a second believe that any of these are the only way. If Islam follows the belief of the Bible and accepts Jesus Christ, then seriously what happened? Did God really send a messenger to be replaced? Did God's word change that quick? Did the Bible not have all the information needed, that the Quran had to be written? I seriously doubt it. How can we have a Bible that is meant to be the word of God and have another book produced shortly afterwards that is the word of God? Surely the creator of all wouldn't need to make amendments, and would have had the foresight to have sent just one message within one book. It doesn't seem logical that the force behind the Universe with all its grandeur could make such a mistake. As we discussed in the introduction, just take into account these three people, each one stands alone, each talks of truth, but how can each talk of truth and yet each teach different things? Could it be the case that we all have our own truth to discover? Remember this book is intended purely as a discussion, Muhammed is the way, Jesus is the way and so is Buddha, these are three individuals who chose not to conform to the belief systems of their time but instead wrote their own truth, from the perspective of their own unique journey. Three individuals that turned off the noise of the world around them and reached within to seek their own personal truth.

What seems to be relevant here is the fact that each of these men chose a unique and personal path, so surely this shows us that conforming to set doctrines set out by others cannot be right for us, and also if you truly want to live a true life then we have to take a leaf out of these men's lives and not follow what is the convention, or worse try and emulate their path, as this again is copying and you are still not going to reveal your 'true self' or the Universal consciousness that is within you and all around you. The greatest gift you were ever given in this life was you. So be you.

It seems that the Universal consciousness has individual messages for us all regarding what our purpose is, and it also seems that there is a recurring message of 'be yourself'.

From this can we say that you should not want to follow any set way? Jesus's way was his own personal truth, and the same goes for Buddha and Muhammed, none of these prophets wanted blood to be spilled in the name of God as is so sadly the case today, in fact the only thing these men have in common was to say that you should do good deeds, shouldn't harm your fellow man and to treat others as you want to be treated. Yet the doctrines of religious practise that have been written post these men living have actually destroyed the true essence of what these people have shown us. What they have shown us is that you should be an individual, you should not conform to other beliefs but find and discover your own truth, even if it takes you your entire life.

This next point shows greatly how dangerously

wrong religion can be with what it preaches. What I am about to say some people will find offensive, especially if you are from a strong religious belief. It needs to be said because it is the truth, and it is a truth that came to me during this journey. It needs to be pointed out because it shows clearly how the touch of man and ego has affected religion based on their own belief and ego.

God created all, therefore God created homosexuals to. If this statement hasn't phased you then that is good. If it has, then that's good to. As this is a profound example of how illogical and blindly led a complex belief system can be. Most major religions condemn homosexuality as a sin and ungodly, and you are clearly on a path to hell if you are homosexual. I was very homophobic when I was younger, I was a 70's child and you never heard about homosexuals in a positive manner. What you did hear though was always negative. And naturally when you are young you tend to have the same thought patterns and beliefs your social background believes. We spoke of this conditioning early in the book.

A few years ago, I was sat in my garden just relaxing and out of nowhere as per usual with this journey, the words popped into my head, 'God created all, if God's work is perfect, and I believe in the evolution of the Universal consciousness and love God, then I must love all my fellow men and women, and embrace their differences, as I would anything else that was God's creation'. It was that simple, and it is that simple.

Homosexuality is not confined to just Humans, animals will also display this behaviour at times, it clearly is part of the design of things. So, if you're sitting reading this and you are from a religious background, and find disgusting what I have written, then know this, you are without realising it condemning, and calling our creator a failure. Who are we to judge? I've even wondered whether nature evolved this way to keep the population of the species down, we just do not know. We are created as we are created, all in the image of God. The trees, the mountains, the ocean, the sunset, the moon, the stars are all the image of God. I hope you can understand what I am saying here, and see the difference between following a set doctrine that has had the human touch exposed to it compared to developing a communication from within, with our creator and consciousness of the Universe, God. When you develop this link the insight comes first hand, the source has not had the human touch or the message tainted.

Let us not get confused here at this point, I'm not saying religion is wrong, if you talk to anyone that is of a religious background, and that truly believes in God and God's judgement then you will find that they are lovely people, people that do not want war or death. Some followers though can appear and come across ignorant at times when in discussion, because questioning their own belief sadly in religion also means to lose faith. A trap found in most religious systems.

Can I add here that I said people that truly believe in God, this doesn't mean Vicars, Reverends, Rabbis, Imams and Priests although there are some of these that are certainly true believers, however just by becoming a part of a religion does not exactly make you behave in a proper fashion. For example, we live in a society where certain religions have shown disgusting behaviour, where leading members of their fold have abused their position of power and harmed adults and children, in physical, mental and sexual ways.

Unfortunately, as with any groups you will always get good contributors and negative contributors but worse than this you can begin to get small minded factions that decipher and misinterpret their chosen religious books to their own means, which sadly results in death for some. The worst-case scenario is occurring right now on this planet, where we see a small extreme branch of a religion maliciously attacking both believers and nonbelievers all the time parading themselves under the banner of religion. What is incredibly sad is that the religion being spoke of here is a very peaceful religion, a religion that teaches not to judge, because if you believe in God and the judgement of God then why should you yourself judge others? I'm not going to mention the religion because it is irrelevant here, what is relevant here though is that we see another example of how following a group can be dangerous, here we have different groups that all believe in God a creator, yet despite this fact, will fight, argue and murder one another over the minor details.

Earlier in this chapter I mentioned that Jesus, Muhammed and Buddha are all the son of God, so please consider what I am about to say. Firstly, close your eyes and imagine what you've been taught to be God, if you're sitting with your eyes closed imagining a human looking 'sky daddy' with flowing white hair and a beard then please I beg you to empty your mind of such trivial content, how can God be a man? Come on let us consider the Universe, is it as a whole, only masculine in nature? No of course not, you would not have the feminine species if this were the case, therefore God cannot be a man type figure, the reason religions have turned God into a masculine figure is to denounce the female role in society, just think about it for a moment, these are books written 1000's of years ago, way before man began to stand shoulder to shoulder with woman.

Another very important point to remember is that time and space did not exist until the Big Bang event, therefore whoever or whatever was responsible for the

Big Bang clearly exists outside the realm of space and time, as it existed prior to the event of creation as we know it. Therefore, the God force cannot be a matter based entity, as matter needs space and time to exist. The God force is beyond our beginning.

So, if the Universe displays masculine and feminine energies then it goes without saying that the God force of the Universe is a harmonious entity of masculine and feminine energy as well as other dualities, i.e. light and dark, bad and good.

Now that we've stopped imagining God looking like Santa in his summer whiteys, we can move forward, the truth is that the God force or God is everywhere. Jesus was the son of God, as was Muhammed as was Buddha and as said earlier so are you. That may be a bit big to swallow, but remember how we discussed earlier how you have been conditioned to seek salvation elsewhere? Conditioned by a money driven society, and if we're honest behind every society there is a religious undertone, therefore we are conditioned even down to the most important connection with what we are, God. Of all the conditioning we receive this is the most damaging, and this is the prime conditioning that actually separates us from the divine power of the Universe. Ironically some followers of religion, seem to have a bigger problem with believers of different faiths, and yet the same people do not seem to have the same feelings regarding nonbelievers. It seems that self-ego is as apparent here within religion, as anywhere else found within the human psyche. It is so wrong to develop the mind frame that 'your way is better than their way', or that 'your God is the true way'. It is here, from this perspective where we find the seedlings of righteousness, difference, superiority and hatred become planted. With the right nurturing and negative conditioning found within some of these sacred righteous groups, these plants will develop and produce the deadliest fruit of all....war!

The argument again it seems coming initially from the perspective of difference rather than embracing their similarities, the belief of God. As a believer in God, life offers so much choice, the Muslims, the Christians, the Hindus, the Mormons, the Jehovah's witnesses, the Sikhs, the Buddhists etc. all proclaim to be the way or the truth. I know we've mentioned this already, but they can't all be the only way. It does seem as mentioned prior that the Universal consciousness truly has spoken through all and that all paths open the door to God.

I truly believe that man alone has destroyed the main messages from the Universal consciousness purely based on their own ego and beliefs based on fear. For instance, why do a few of these religions claim to be the only way? You will hear Christians say 'Jesus is the only way to God', and that you must accept Christ to avoid hell. Islam displays the same concept only this time Muhammed has to be accepted as the final prophet and the way to God.

Therefore, righteousness in one's faith, rather than just simple love and a faith solely in God is separating you from your fellow man, and yet if you are a Muslim, there is a good chance that if you were born into a Christian family, you would be as devout just under the different title of Christian, the same applies to a Christian with a different fate and born into a Muslim family.

These religions that proclaim to be the only way, also use fear as a resourceful tool. Where each will put fear into the minds of its followers by saying if you deny such a faith you are destined for hell. It truly baffles me that some religions refer to God as he, or the Father. So, when you do not follow your particular religions 'way', the image that is given is of an angry male all powerful force that hands down judgement. Rather than the loving harmonious connected force it truly is.

So here is my question to any Muslims, Christians, Catholics, Jehovah's witnesses etc. If your way is the only way, then what about people who live in lands far, far away, that far that neither of the main religions have reached there yet. How about other planets? Are they all destined to hell? Of course not. If any of the main religions were the only way, then none of the other religions would have ever developed. And the message would have always been the same. Our diversity comes from the fact that the 'truth' has been spoken in different languages, at different times. All with similar themes but differing stories.

So, embrace your differences from your fellow man, even more importantly embrace your similarities. It is only the combined effort of us as a whole that can change the way this planet is. All the time spent fighting and fussing over small details takes the time away from us that is needed to change the world forever, for our children, and our children's children. If anything, you should step away from the egotistical aspect of your religion, it only places you within a box of confinement that can separate you from your fellow human. And in the worst case separate you from a fellow believer based solely on a difference of opinion over the 'minor' details.

To follow no set belief system is fine. Believe me, you can talk inwardly to God, even outwardly. You can meditate and contemplate the meaning of your entire existence in places where you can see and feel God's presence, like outside sitting in the natural world around you. I find God in these places; the stars, the ocean, beautiful landscapes, in fact anywhere outside where the world is as nature had intended it to be. I'm no hippy, I also see God, the Universal consciousness in the field of art, science, music and creativity, even within the realm of sport. The human experience expands and becomes greater as the Universal consciousness itself expands and grows, we are God's work in action, our actions good or bad will create and creation is God's work.

I have walked into religious buildings and felt nothing, yet I have felt awe when looking out of an airplane at 33,000ft and seeing a landscape of clouds, all dancing in different tones to a setting summer sun. I'd much rather contemplate all, and chat and be thankful to God here. Plus, these places, are an ideal place to sit eyes closed and visualise and see yourself as the person you would want to be, more loving, more understanding, more you. Here is the place where you order from the Universe what you so desire. Here is the realm of creation.

There are a few truths regarding religion. The first, you do not need to go to church or any other so called 'house of God' for worship or even to connect, you are already connected, on a level that certainly does not need the confines of a material based fancy building. Think about it, wouldn't you feel closer to God whilst strolling through a field, or along a beautiful beach? Or simply looking up at the sky on a clear night, seeing the stars and knowing each one is a solar system with its own unique neighbourhood of planets, truly taking in all the glory of the Universe around you? I certainly feel as though I am walking alongside my creator in these scenarios, although the connection is everywhere, literally. There truly is no divide between you, me and the Universal consciousness, God. This will be made a lot clearer in later chapters.

Secondly, there is no 'go between' needed and definitely no saviour to follow. A lot of religions use a saviour as a rule of thumb to compare one's own life to.

Why should you compare yourself to a person that lived during a different time period? Why live the way someone lived over a thousand years ago? The world was different then, society was different. How do these ways relate at all to modern day living? They simply do not. The Universe grows and evolves as do we. Old ways have no place in new beginnings.

The final truth is the biggest and the saddest. Religion, or people waving the banner of it for their own needs have been responsible for the deaths of millions. And this is no weak statement, this is the truth. The true good people of religion I believe would be just as good if they had never had the conditioning of religion. Good people do not come from one perfect section of society, good people come from all walks of life, there are truly good and bad in all regardless of religious background.

Now I know through conversations that when some people consider a belief in an entity they can't see, they naturally struggle, also because God has sadly been given the role of 'wish-maker' and 'saviour' to our struggles in society so, again it's easy to see why the God figure that has been created has fallen short. You will hear people say that God cannot exist because of wars and suffering, because of ill health and disease. The truth is, it is ourselves that should be held responsible for any wars on this planet. It is ourselves that can ease the pain of others suffering by OUR actions, it is us through living healthier that can ease our own suffering. The Universe in which we live is cruel, life and death repeatedly plays out second after second, from the smallest single cell organism, right up to stars and solar systems being completely devoured by a black hole. Everything it seems has to die. Death it seems is as significant to our existence as life itself.

Why have we been conditioned to seek salvation

elsewhere when we can clearly help ourselves? It is this unfortunate perception of God that has led many to quite simply not believe any more. The truth is that the Universal consciousness is the creator and the beginning of everything, its force is omnipotent, and that is it, and like anything created, the Universe has a purpose, as we are children of the Universe then we have a purpose to, which individually through taking on life with love, gratitude and compassion, and releasing our conditioned content we will slowly reveal what that purpose is.

Once we accept the responsibilities of being creators, we can then move forward and become the change needed. All religion and mass media social conditioning has done is make us look elsewhere for strength, made us worship mortal men, when all the time we are all the children of God, the air, the creatures, the trees, the grass, the sky, the planets, the sun, the galaxies, are all God's creation, and are God itself, created.

We view a tree as being a part of nature, the clouds, the air, the wildlife, all of it, but ask yourself do you see yourself as being a part of it? Do you see yourself as a child of Earth? Of the Universe? Or are you just John or Jane Doe, a matter based being, inert from your creator and the greatness of this Universe? If your thinking does it really matter? Then Yes! It matters more than anything. How sad is the mindset of the media conditioned, that scurries around doing chore after chore, serving a system of materialistic gain, believing "God does not exist, I'm alive and when I die that's it". This mindset is so self destructive to our soul as it is so far from the truth.

We are magnificent beings, information holders of our ancestry, the library being held in the DNA department, we are evolved stardust, and billions of years of evolution has bought us here, and we are all truly one and all truly connected, better than any Wi-Fi connection you can imagine. We are the rulers of our own Universe, and our potential is only locked by our own thought patterns. This is where I stand, this is where I know I am in the Universe, and this beyond anything else empowers me to wake every day, with a smile and urgency to challenge the day before me. Where all aspects of my life are an opportunity, and never an obligation.

Now I know that whatever your standpoint on religion is, God etc. It is going to come from your own personal perspective based on your own 'content' or consciousness, some believe some don't. I hope that by the end of this book you will know without doubt that you are of a higher calling and that you are significant and that you are one part of a conscious whole that makes up everything from here to the vast edge of our Universe and all the spaces in between. More importantly the Universe or God wants you to be you and only you, no imitations no copycats but 'you', as the Universe had always intended you to be, for this is how the Universe evolves and continually self learns. Go and watch any nature documentary and you will see how clever the Universe and nature's design is. If scientifically we can all agree that nature is clever in its evolution and plan of action, then why would God have been wrong in your design? If you don't believe in God, then a simple rephrasing will suffice. Why would nature have been wrong in your design? It clearly can't be.

Now we've begun to consider God and religion let us consider the atheist's leading argument against the creation of the Universe, evolution.

Firstly, evolution does not oppose a belief in God, evolution opposes the creation story of most religions. If we take for example the opening book of the Bible, Genesis. I've had a good read of Genesis and honestly speaking, it clearly doesn't mention key facts about Earth's long history, for example the prehistoric era doesn't get a mention at all, only Adam and Eve, and most are familiar with this tale of how God took a rib from Adam to create Eve as told in the Old testament part of the Bible. As entertaining as this story is, it is still clearly a story, as archaeological digs have unsurfaced our ancestors, both Homosapiens and even a small percentage of the globe sharing DNA with other bipedal's like Neanderthal man.

    I stand by the theory of evolution, it clearly explains how we got here through billions of years of evolution, it certainly doesn't denounce a creator, as with anything even the evolution of our Universe had a start point. Evolution best explains the work in progress of the Universal consciousness, God. However, the Father of Evolution Charles Darwin did not have all the answers. Charles Darwin's theory of evolution has holes in it to.

    For instance, Charles Darwin puts forward the idea that life arose through spontaneous creation, for example if you make a mud puddle in your garden eventually the environment will produce the right conditions to create frogs, or another example rotting meat will create maggots. Later scientists through tests in clean sterile labs discovered that you can leave a piece of rotting meat in a sterile air tight container and maggots will never spontaneously appear. There are other factors needed like the fly, to come and land on the meat and lay its eggs. Life does not spontaneously create in an inert environment, there are other factors needed for life on a microbiological scale as scientists later proved, in fact, nothing has ever spontaneously created anything!

    Can you see how silly it is to believe that anything can come from nothing? Life does not just appear, and this is true of life on Earth, and true regarding the start point of the Universe itself.

Sadly, though Darwin did not have access to the information known today, so even though evolution theory is part right it still brings man no closer to the question 'how did life arise on this planet, or in the Universe at all?! We will get to this later in the book.

Back to evolution, the common belief system of this planet now is that the creation of the Universe came from a Big Bang and this theory has now slowly been proven to be right, with vast telescopes looking that deep into space that there are images seen of our Universe shortly after the Big Bang began, and when I say shortly after the event we're not talking minutes, hours or days, but rather 1/100th of a second after the event had begun. Some of you will probably be thinking, 'How does looking deep into space show us how the Universe began?' This is achieved through the speed of light, and how long it takes the light to arrive here over the vast expanse of space, for example if you looked at a planet that was 100 million light years away then you would be seeing the planet as it was 100 million years ago, because it has taken the light 100 million years travelling at the speed of light to get here. Here's an interesting fact; if you stood on a planet that was 100 million light years away and pointed a telescope powerful enough to reach Earth then what you would see would be surprising, because in theory you would get front row tickets to the prehistoric era, watching dinosaurs roam the Earth. We do truly live in a bizarre and compelling Universe.

So, after all the years of debate religion had it right, there clearly was a creation point of time, matter and space. Now science can confirm this fact with the Big Bang theory, does this mean that the God force cannot exist? Because another unfortunate part of social conditioning that we have already discussed is the sad belief that 'if you believe in science you can't believe in God'. Truthfully? Of course, not, it merely defends the notion of a God force. The truth is that before Edwin Hubble put forward the notion of the 'Big Bang' theory in 1929, many scientists had as already discussed and put forward the theory that space had always been there and that it was inert and would stay in the same state forever. I believe this theory may have been put forward because it stands opposed to a creator. By theorising that it was forever and never changing, they would never have to ask the most puzzling question of all, which is how it all began. Science will always struggle with the subject matter of God, let's be honest science loves to quantify units of the Universe so that it can understand them, how can science with such a number based system ever factor in the 'God force'. You can't quantify the unquantifiable. But science can confirm God's work. That is the only way one could ever describe the workings of this Universe as we discover and learn new things.

    Only living organisms learn, and learn from their own mistakes. Look at nature and evolution and tell me the Universe isn't self-learning. Nature always gets better, replacing older, useless ways. So now tell me that the Universe isn't alive.

    Therefore, science has looked for ways and theories to negate a creator, however as some physicists will say themselves today, 'God' is the only explanation that holds true to the creation of the Universe, because no other factor can justify or seem to fill that part of the equation at all.

    The fact is that scientists now believe that in a trillionth of a second a subatomic particle expanded to the size of the sun during the Big Bang, this was the rate of acceleration. If that doesn't sound a lot consider this, you can fit 1.3 million Earth's inside the sun, and that should make anyone think 'wow!' But here's the question to anybody that still may think that God or a creator does not exist: we know energy cannot spontaneously appear, energy is converted, that is, you have to put something in to get something out. For example, a kettle requires electrical energy which in turn it converts to heat energy, so my question to the scientific thinker is this. The energy for the Big Bang was huge, immense, in fact that big that space is still expanding 14 billion years after the event, so where did this energy come from? Interestingly all the energy present in the Universe now was present at the beginning point of the Big Bang.

So, did the Universe really do the impossible and create itself from nothingness? Science and the laws of physics say no. What we also know is that time itself was created at the exact same point as the Universe began, so as mentioned earlier, whatever started this event exists outside the realms of time, space and matter. Could this be consciousness? Scientific evidence points this way.

Consciousness is not matter based, nor time fixed, and it seems is not held down by space. Our own consciousness can recall past, look at the present and create our future. Our consciousness when sleeping and in the dream state can take us places we have never seen, make us meet people we've never met in reality, and also connect us with past loved ones no longer here on the material plane (if you have lost a loved one and then dreamt of them you find that the dream feels so real. In fact, in that moment it is real). Therefore, it is fair to assume that our consciousness is the same as the Universal consciousness; it has no bounds, no time, space or material restrictions, and is at the basis of the creation of our Universe, and was at the source of our creation, it is consciousness that is there from birth, and that which departs the body on death, leaving the matter based time restricted body behind.

Theoretical physicists are now looking into this question of where the energy came from for the Big Bang and no doubt in the near future will answer this question and discover what was before the Big Bang, however what this should serve us to do is to show just how far the mind of humanity has expanded. It isn't too long ago that humanity believed that the Earth was flat and that if you took your vessel onto the sea and sailed for long enough eventually you would fall off the edge of the world, now centuries later we are aware that the Earth is round and much more, to the point of understanding the creation of the Universe in which we live, so once theoretical physicists discover what came before the Big Bang no doubt the question will arise of what came before that! If we are the only beings like ourselves in the Universe, then we are the first time that the matter based Universe has evolved to a point to consciously look back on itself and question its own beginnings.

All this information should hopefully start to change your mindset into one that is realising the Universe that you are a part of is much more complex and deeper than you could ever imagine. And that also and quite unfortunately our understanding has been unclear from the start.

If the Universe was created and nothing is created without purpose, then what is the purpose of the Universe? And as we're of the Universe what is our purpose?'

Regarding purpose, it is the same for all and this is covered in the final chapter. Even though the overall purpose is the same for all, our own individual purposes are all very different. This then begs the next question, "How do I hear the Universe?" Or "How do I know my own purpose?"

The truth is you already know all the answers that you have ever needed, your soul and consciousness have always known, however with the restraints of the material domain in which we live placed on us we slowly forget how to listen to the Universe or God. Quietening down the outside world helps massively in discovering your own purpose. Background noise in any aspect of life will always cloud you.

Now remember at the beginning of this chapter I mentioned how I firmly know that God or a god force that brings life to the Universe exists?

It may seem contrary to speak of God and at the same time give a negative view on the possible problems with religion. I believe that most reading this will probably feel the same, religion is another term or classification that causes divides between the people. It is no different to a social class, ethnic grouping, or any other invisible barrier that separates us the people from one another. And, it is this mindset that restrains us, keeps us in the dark and ultimately leads to a diminished existence. Personally, I have no colour, no race and definitely no set religion, I am human and my home town is Earth, and I am connected to all in the Universe because the Universe made me and everything else within it.

How many people do you know think with this clear mindset? Not many, because quite honestly society has orchestrated it all this way. As mentioned already it is the simple rule of 'divide and conquer', and it is this that is played out every day amongst us the people. The media magnifies it all too well, society emphasises all our cultural differences and the masses play along fighting wars over their differences. What a different world it would be, if for just once we stopped and tried something a little different and compared our similarities rather than our differences. I know on reflection after comparing our similarities we would discover as humans regardless of colour or creed we have a lot more similarities than we do differences, in fact, the only significant differences are matters of the mind, or as I mentioned previously, matters of our own content or consciousness. If we changed our content, and consciousness then I have no doubt that the world as a whole would be a brighter, healthier and safer place indeed.

If we consider similarities in religion and take a close look, we sometimes discover little gems of knowledge handed down from the Universal consciousness or God, to individuals to be passed on. Little synchronicities found between religions. The first little synchronicity will be discussed in the next chapter. The second synchronicity will be discussed in the Chapter on the 33, 333 phenomena.

Chapter 5

The Pine Cone.

There is a symbol seen in some religions dating back to antiquity and it is the pine cone. Below are several images, some are from several different religions, some from different ages of antiquity up until present day belief systems. See what you think.

Figure 1. Pine cone on the Staff of Osiris, Egyptian Museum Turino, Italy.

Figure 2. Pine cone Vatican city

Figure 3. Relief of Marduk the Babylonian God holding the pine cone in his right hand.

Figure 4. Lord Shiva with his hair resembling the pine cone.

Figure 5. Buddha statue. Again it is the head/ hair region that displays the pine cone.

So now you've seen these images clearly displaying a pine cone, the Catholics with their 12-foot pine cone in the centre of the Vatican, Shiva and Buddha both with heads shaped like a pine cone. What do you make of them? Or the Pine cone on the staff of Osiris? From these examples, we find that the pine cone has been used in artwork, architecture and other forms from Indonesia, Babylon, Christianity and the Romans.

The pine cone semiotics cannot be there as some strange accidental coincidence. I believe it is a clue that points directly to opening your own conversation with God or the Universe whichever one you wish to call it. And all these cultures and religious beliefs whether knowingly or not are quite clearly sharing something the same.

The pine cone I believe is a direct reference to the Pineal gland which sits in the middle of the brain, and it is here that many now believe consciousness resides, or as some people call it, your 'mind's eye' or third eye.

This isn't solely referenced with the pine cone; other cultures use the 'Bindi' dot which references the third eye also. This dot worn by Sikhs, Hindus and seen on any statue of Buddha is another direct reference to the third eye. But why then, you may ask is a pine cone used? Simply put the pine cone resembles the pineal gland and secondly has the mathematics of the creator's mark, as it's a direct example of the 'Divine Proportion'. We will cover the divine proportion in the next chapter.

The Pineal gland is interesting as scientific studies show the right and left hemispheres of the brain have separate functions yet the uniqueness of the pineal gland is that it sits dead centre. This is a link to your spiritual self, a link to consciousness and its connection to the Universe or God. It is here where you shall find your 'true self' and discover own your purpose.

In Theosophy (a collection of the mystical and occult philosophies concerning the nature of divinity, and the origin of the Universe) the third eye is related to the pineal gland. The third eye refers to the gate that leads to inner realms and the spaces of higher consciousness.

There is another way that religions seem to be connected. This connection seems to come through the form of numbers. These numbers are used repeatedly in some religions and secret societies. However, there are a set of numbers that a lot of cultures call Master numbers, and these seem very significant indeed. Numbers are the only universal language, and this will be explored in a later chapter.

Why were we not showed this in religious studies at school? Why, when we are taught so much about the differences between the religions, are we not showed the continuities? People often struggle with religion because of its opposing factor...religion! I wonder that if we the people were shown the continuities, for example the fact that most religions talk of a creator, and the fact that all religions seem to point and reference the spiritual side of man with the reference to the pine cone, and that there seems to be an underlying mathematical language found within nature, then maybe the worldly viewpoint of God would change.

As previously said there is a second reference within the pine cone and it's a mathematical one that we as humans have been aware of for a long long time, the pine cone itself holds the key to the nature and the design of our Universe, as the pine cone is a perfect example of the 'Divine proportion' or the 'Golden mean'. This beautiful phenomenon which is not by any means a random mathematical number (as the world around us displays it everywhere, and I mean everywhere!) points without any doubt to an intelligent design to our Universe, and simply put if a design format can be deemed intelligent then something intelligent had to put it there. Remember this is a discussion between myself and you the reader, it is by no means any form of an authority, but at this point if you are standing here as a nonbeliever then surely these facts were not known to you, is it not compelling that despite its own entrapments, religion had the creation of the Universe correct? Is it not compelling to see religions using identical iconography that point to not only consciousness and our creator but also to the design of our Universe? Maybe, maybe not, let's continue.

When I use the term intelligently designed I mean

exactly that, for instance to see intelligence we need to see patterns, set rules, set laws. Surely if we can find design in our own cosmos then surely, we can find our own acceptance of a creator?

Have you ever stopped and stared at an amazing piece of architecture, an oil painting maybe or even listened to a beautiful piece of music? Well have you ever thought for a moment that they just appeared, spontaneously from nowhere like magic? No, of course you haven't, when you look and see the art, architecture or hear the music you know that it has been created because of its composition, you know by its being that it is not just an accident, because any of these creative examples require consciousness and a complicated process to achieve. Keeping this in mind, step outside at night and look up at the stars in the sky. Take a deeper look, and view images of planets, of galaxies, or nebulae; which are described as galactic nurseries, as these are where stars are born. Watch any nature documentary. How can anyone look at such beautiful views and not wonder just for a moment how clever it all is. Are we really to believe that the Universe and how it works so intricately to create life, just happened?

Even modern day physicists say that our Universe is a miracle of existence with no room for error in any of its defining laws. It is that finely tuned that the modern scientific theory now to denounce a creator is that we live in a multiverse, where millions of universes would exist but we live in the winning lottery of universes where the accidental universe somehow got it right. Of course, this is a ridiculous atheist notion. Even the greatest minds of our time are scratching their heads at the intricate nature of our Universe and still we plod forward denying what seems to become clearer and clearer in the abyss for the truth.

The execution, mechanism, function and design of this Universe is not an accident, it is a masterpiece of knowledge, understanding and infinite intelligence or as some would believe, it accidentally just happened.
If a simple small item such as a painting needs a creator, then how can we possibly presume that all this just happened?

The Universe isn't a simple system, it is intelligently designed and we shall look at this in the following chapter.

Chapter 6

The Mark Of The Creator, Intelligent Design.

The Universe around us is exploding with intelligent design and the creator's mark is everywhere, just look at DNA and the coding sequence. Lots of researchers into this field even say themselves that for something to be coded then something intelligent had to put the code there. Just think about any piece of coded information you may have seen, if you track backwards from the information to the source you always find intelligence, someone has to put the code there. As humans, certain key changes seem to take place at certain points in our lives, from crawling to talking and walking, right through to adolescence and beyond, it is clear that our DNA is programmed. The programming is that easily identifiable scientists are able to genetically modify food, and even clone animals all solely from DNA.

From four separate building blocks, our body manufactures everything it needs by simply arranging these four components into different sequences. Our DNA is programmed containing tons of information and is more powerful than any cutting edge modern day computer. Regarding information transfer, scientists say that the transfer of information that occurs when a sperm fertilises an egg is huge, and that it would take hundreds of powerful computers working side by side to achieve such a transfer of information.

It is interesting that statistically you couldn't put a number on the odds of the Universe at all evolving by accident, especially when these extremely complicated codes are present throughout the DNA of life because it is impossible, in fact statistically the odds are much lower that the Universe was created, compared to the odds of the Universe being an accident. Is this not one example of intelligent design, a coded system that brings life into existence?

Or how about the 'Golden mean', 'Divine proportion' or 'Phi' as it's known which we began to touch upon in the previous chapter with the pine cone, a ratio 1:1.618 that occurs throughout nature, a code which is that prevalent within the architecture of the Universe that it earned the title the 'Divine proportion'. If you are not aware of this ratio then let me tell you that it is everywhere in the Universe and it is all around you, and even within you. Scientists have discovered that this proportion is found in leaves, shells, trees, flowers, human bone structure, DNA, in galaxy formations and it truly is prevalent everywhere. Interestingly the nearer something conforms to this ratio the more beautiful it appears, as it is more naturally appealing to the eye. Artists have been aware of this ratio for centuries, artists like Leonardo da Vinci who used it regularly in his practise with the premise of making his works more appealing to the viewer.

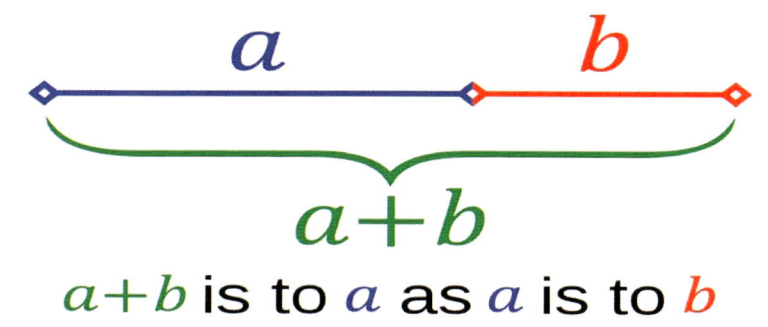

$a+b$ is to a as a is to b

Figure 6. The Golden ratio (phi) as a line.

Below is a Nautilus shell, its design best shows the

pattern of nature and as shown in the following image, its connection to the Fibonacci series of numbers.

Figure 7 Nautilus shell.

    Interestingly the commercial world have used this ratio for years, using it in the 'A' series of paper you use daily, A4 A3 A2 A1 all conform to the ratio of 'phi', book size, magazines, and even credit cards have all been manufactured to conform to this ratio, and why? Because this ratio appeals to us, we are created with the same design principles, so naturally we're attracted to the same design principles.

    The ratio is 1:1.618 and it is not just a random number that scientists have looked for, more it's a number that was clearly 'noticed', through studies of nature. So, any sceptic that may be sitting at home thinking you could find any mathematical number ratio occurring more than once in the Universe, think again, because there is no other ratio so prevalent in you or the world around you.

Please feel free to take time out from this book and go and read around the subject, there are plenty of great books on this subject from the maths section to the spiritual section in any good book shop, and a whole array of websites and forums online.

What makes the divine proportion so interesting is that its ratio is created from the Fibonacci series of numbers. Without going off subject and turning this discussion into a maths lesson I will try to make this short and simple.

Starting with 0 then 1 so 0, 1 we then get the next number by adding the previous two numbers, so 0+1=1. Therefore, the next number in the series is 1. So, we have 0, 1, 1 then carrying this trend on we get 0, 1, 1, 2 then 3 then 5 then 8 and so on, making the Fibonacci sequence 0, 1, 2, 3, 5, 8, 13, 21, 34, 55, 89, 144, 233, 377, etc.

As you start to go up into the Fibonacci sequence and then divide any number in the sequence with the previous number you get the divine ratio 1.618. This begins at 89 divided by 55 = 1.618   Taking the next numbers 144 divided by 89 = 1.617977 (close enough). The next numbers 233 divided by 144 = 1.618 and finally 377 divided by 233 =1.618 this carries on right through the Fibonacci series.

Here is the Fibonacci series as a drawing, see how similar it is to the shell, in fact see how it is exactly the same blue print of the Nautilus shell. This is mathematically nature's design.

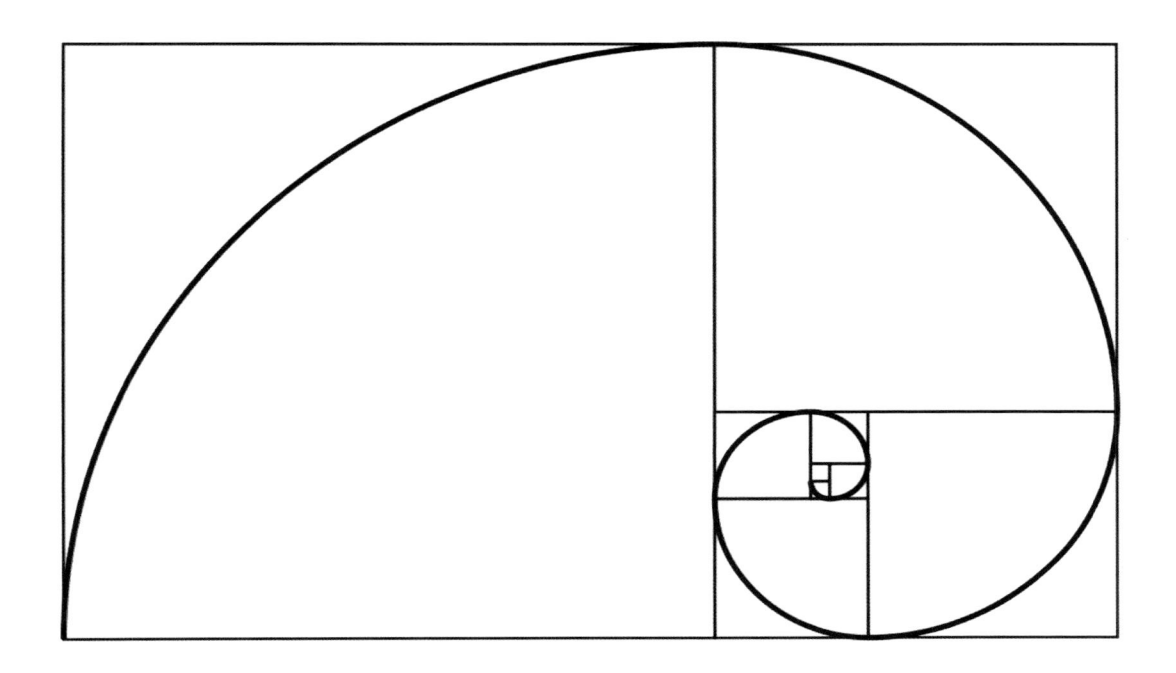

Figure 8. Fibonacci series as a drawing.

There are literally a Universe full of examples of how this one particular ratio seems to pop up everywhere, is it a coincidence? Or is this another example of the higher intelligence that binds us all together? Below are a few more examples of the divine proportion in nature. Take a look and see if you can notice a clear pattern of design.

Figure 9. Phi in plants.

Figure 10. Phi in leaf formation.

Figure 11. Phi used in Art. Here displayed on Leonardo da Vinci', Mona Lisa.

There are tons of examples and this information is certainly enlightening when you see clear defined laws and patterns in the design of our Universe, and these laws are so defined that the universal laws can be seen on a smaller scale that reflect the same principle with larger entities of our Universe, for example let us consider a tree. On its grandest scale, we see a tree fully grown, with its strong trunk, branches and leaves, however when you look at how the trunk separates to form smaller branches, then these branches separate at different points to create even smaller branches then eventually we're left with the leaf. And on the leaf, you see a pattern where the smallest structure is simply a sized down version of the whole, look at a small twig and see how it goes from thick to thin at the end and how smaller branches come from it, it's a smaller scaled down version of the whole. Other examples of this phenomenon can be seen in nature with arteries, veins and capillaries respectively being scaled down smaller versions of the former, we call this phenomenon 'Fractals'. So, what is a fractal? A fractal is a never-ending pattern, where the whole resembles the smallest unit and the smallest unit resembles the whole. Fractals are infinitely complex patterns that are self-similar across different scales. They are created by repeating a simple process over and over in an ongoing feedback loop. Creating infinity within a finite area, fractals continually repeat the creator's mark.

Interestingly our Universe is fractal by design, even right down to atomic structure, the design of our Universe clearly shows patterns of design that clearly work. My favourite example of a fractal that is truly mind blowing is when you consider an atom and the solar system. An atom has a central nucleus containing neutrons and protons and in orbit around the nucleus are electrons all whizzing around at the speed of light.

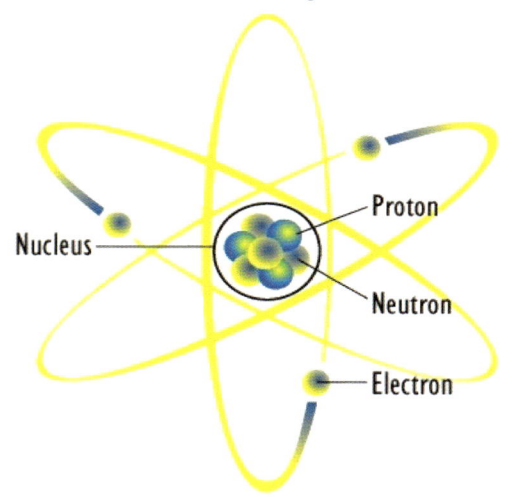

Figure 12. Diagram of an atom (Rutherford Model).

With this model of an atom in your mind, consider the solar system, think of the Sun and the planets in their own individual orbits, is this not a repeating design? Where the same blueprint of design is applied on both an atomic level and an interplanetary solar level? Is this not evidence of how connected our Universe is? Are we not seeing the same orbiting structure exhibited in the Sun and in the nucleus of an atom? What is extremely interesting here is that protons are found in the nucleus and are positively charged so therefore they give the nucleus of an atom a positive charge, it has been discovered that the surface of our Sun also has a positive charge. Orbiting the atom are negatively charged electrons, and orbiting our Sun are planets, and our own planet Earth has a negative surface charge. I am not suggesting these electro-forces hold the solar system in place, as there are other forces at work such as gravity, but it is still all the same compelling.

    Galaxies are made up of billions of stars, billions of stars all rotating around a centre point, very much like the planets that revolve around our own star. So again, we see the same design but now on a larger scale. It is now understood that at the centre of each galaxy you will find a huge black hole with its massive gravitational pull creating spin, and causing the stars to rotate around in an orbit. At the centre of an atom we can also find this same force, as it has been discovered that the centre of an atom as the same black hole energy, and it is this gravitational force that causes the electrons to spin around the nucleus, so here again we can see a clearly defined design that resonates from beyond a microscopic view right up to the heavens that we can admire with a telescope, the design is clearly present everywhere.

Figure 13. The Solar system.

It is interesting to note that it was Earnest Rutherford that first proposed the model of the atom in 1910 and that he clearly noticed this similarity.

6. *The electrons revolve round the nucleus with high velocities to counterbalance the electrostatic forces of attraction between protons and electrons. Rutherford's atomic model resembles the planetary motion in solar system. Therefore, Rutherford's model of an atom was called planetary model.*

In the fractal Universe in which we live you will truly find the Universe within a grain of sand, and there are many more interesting discoveries regarding how our Universe works in an intelligent fashion, however I chose to mention the examples I did as these were familiar and incredibly intriguing to myself when I was first made aware of them. However, I will mention one more example, and this is Cymatics.

Cymatics is the study of frequency on apparent inert matter. For example, take a crystal glass, when you look at it, it seems inert and just a piece of moulded glass. However, when you play sound at a high enough pitch something begins to happen. The glass will start to wobble and once the correct pitch is achieved the glass will shatter. This shows us two things; the first is that although we perceive the glass to be inert and solid, it clearly isn't and secondly, there seems to be unseen forces at work on a smaller level that become disrupted by sound.

From our second conclusion, we can see that everything seems to be held together by frequency or sound, and we see this in the case of the crystal glass by how its subatomic particles become disrupted by a change in frequency.

What conclusions can we draw so far from this discussion? The first is that if a creator or God doesn't exist then the Universe appeared from nothing and out of nowhere, a spontaneous creation with no creator, and with it sprang an unfolding, random, accidental process that bought stability to itself in that it self-maintained and steadily grew, whilst growing creating conditions for life to appear and at the same time doing it so accidentally perfect. In fact, that accidentally perfect that for it to have had any chance of happening at all in its first attempt, several other millions of universes had to also appear out of nowhere from nothingness; remember the modern day scientific theory of how the multiverse exists and how we must live on the winning ticket version of all possible universes? And all this happened without any purpose as it is fair to assume that anything deemed accidental has no purpose in life.

Alternatively, we can start to see what is evident all around us; the Universe we live in is designed on a magnificent scale, a scale of which today's scientists with today's technology, still only grasp the smallest of understanding. A design with a visible blue print found in the 'Divine proportion' and coding systems found within the biology of life. A Universe that could not exist at all if any of the physical laws within it were slightly changed. This Universe is no accident and neither are you.

We can keep the viewpoint if you like that the Universe appeared from nothing and that's fine. From this we can keep with the idea that life sprung up somewhere at some point and never know the answer how, because as already discussed Darwin's theory never did answer that one riddle, how did life suddenly appear from matter? And more specifically how did consciousness and thought arise out of the vast matter of time and space that is our very own reality? And remember that on our own little home of Earth, life hasn't just sprung up once but twice. Many millions of years ago all was wiped out when a massive meteor hit. The dominant life of that time was eradicated, some instantly, some later due to the drastic change of conditions on Earth. Shortly afterwards a new dominant life evolved, and here we are standing and living alongside a whole array of other intelligent life from the animal kingdom. Our planet and the Universe around truly is a wondrous thing and it is capable of creating life not just once on this planet but twice, after having its environment changed drastically by a meteor hitting many millions of years ago.

Chapter 7

Everything Is Connected And Everything Is One.

We were discussing at the end of the previous chapter about how science has never answered the riddle of how life suddenly sprang up in the Universe. So, when did the first smallest single cellular organism develop from what seems apparent lifeless matter?

We discussed how the noncreationist views the Universe as being some kind of anomaly, an accident, and that from an atheist's perspective we are merely evolved bacteria hurtling through time and space with no governed purpose. Even though as we have already discussed everything has a purpose, from the Sun in our sky providing life to our solar system, to the trees producing oxygen for us to breathe, everything it seems has a purpose, and everything is in a constant state of evolution. Evolution is key to our very being, and is exactly why we are given the role of creator within our own lives. I have already mentioned this but I want to mention this point again. We as humans will not be around forever, at some point we will be replaced, maybe like the dinosaurs were through a natural disaster, maybe through evolution, maybe even wiped out by ourselves. Only one thing is certain, humanity as with everything else within the Universe is a transitory state. The Universe views the world and learns through our eyes, therefore being creative ensures development. Development of consciousness, development of life itself. Evolution is not separate from Gods work, evolution is the result of the learning of the 'Universal consciousness', God. As it evolves so does the Universe itself.

Anyway, let's move on, so we had a 'Big bang' almost 14 billion years ago, and conventional old school science books teach us that from this Big bang matter slowly took form shaping the stars and then the planets. Then on these planets, inert particles of matter evolved into bacteria which eventually evolved and became advanced life and the evolution carried on right up to this day. This theory is great as it is substantiated with clear scientific research, however does this answer all questions? It certainly explains our matter based history of the Universe. The question it still doesn't address is, 'how did life suddenly arise?' And the second question I want you to consider is 'where did consciousness come from?' Because the matter based theory of evolution suggests that life spontaneously came after years of evolution of simple chemicals becoming compounds that in turn evolved to become bacteria. And that life somehow sprang out of nowhere from evolved non-living matter. I don't know about you but if the Universe is merely inert matter then inert matter surely cannot ever evolve into a conscious living being? Could inert matter eventually evolve enough to 'think' and 'be'? Well it can't, therefore something in this theory is wrong, as life does not ever spontaneously arise.

The problem is that these former theories were all built on a scientific standpoint that the Universe is matter based, when actually it is far from that. The truth is that physicists have known this for some time and many of you reading this may know that the Universe around you, that we see, feel and touch as a matter based reality is in fact not truly solid, in fact it's not solid at all, we perceive the Universe as solid because of our own levels of perception, and yet we now know that materials are constructed from compounds, and that on a smaller level these compounds can be broken down into individual elements and that these elements Hydrogen, Helium, Oxygen etc. can be dissected down further into protons, neutrons and electrons, and now in this age of science even these atomic particles can be broken down even smaller into subatomic particles, with subatomic particles being the basis of study for Quantum Physicists. Interestingly it was Earnest Rutherford that discovered that the inside of an atom is actually 99.9999999999999% empty space, that means you and I on a subatomic level are also 99.9999999999999% empty space, so in fact we're definitely not solid at all!

    So now we know that the world in fact isn't solid and from this we can see that the Universe itself isn't, as these subatomic particles that make up you and I, are the same subatomic particles found in everything on the Earth, right up to the stars and galaxies and all the spaces in-between. You may sit there and think 'OK then but why is this at all relevant?' It is relevant because now you should see that the Universe is a mass of subatomic particles all connected as a whole by frequency yet separated as individuals by frequency. To prove everything is one quantum physics tells us that if you change the frequency of one subatomic particle then all other subatomic particles in the entire Universe will change their frequency to accommodate for this change, and from this quantum physics shows us that the Universe is not a materialistic inert based environment, but is in actuality all interconnected, to the point where the tiniest change on the smallest subatomic particle affects the whole.

    From this we should be able to conclude that we're not just evolved bacteria living on a huge rock speeding through space at a great speed that by some pure chance and coincidence evolved to form life as we know it. In fact, we are not separate from the Earth at all, because the Earth is made up of exactly the same subatomic particles too and even the space in between, from our Sun to the outer planets and beyond, it truly is all one and all interconnected.

Remember we touched upon fractals and intelligent design in the last chapter. Well it seems that apart from the Universe being able to create infinity within a finite area and that a clear design pattern to the Universe is present, there also seems to be an interconnectivity beyond the fastest broadband known today or ever in the future. As subatomic particles don't comply with the normal rules of space, matter and time these signals are instantaneous, so instantaneous that time could not be used to measure. This evidence best exemplifies the omnipotent power of the Universal consciousness, God.

It seems the Universe is capable of instantaneous signals between itself as a whole, and creates itself as it grows with mathematical precision as demonstrated by phi and its fractal repeating tendencies. If this were any other subject other than that of our creator, then the evidence would point clearly towards an architect, a very informed architect, an architect that exists outside matter, space and time itself, and this level of creation would be too intricate and therefore deemed ridiculous to think it just happened.

So, if the Universe isn't just a matter based world, what is it? And equally important, what's holding it all together to give these particles separation, shape and form? To answer this question we need to delve a little deeper into the world of quantum physics.

A few decades ago quantum physicists performed a double slit experiment (a light beam fired through a sheet with two slits onto a background to see where the particles/waves hit) with quantum particles, or more precisely photons of light. What they discovered astounded them.

When the laser beam was on and when the photons were not observed, the photons turned into a wave pattern, but once they were observed again they behaved like particles again, so what did this mean? If the subatomic particles behaved like a wave when no one was viewing but turned into particles once viewed then it could only mean one thing; it meant that the particles responded to a conscious observer, and that there was an interaction between the particles and the watcher, therefore it is concluded that the Universe responds and reacts to consciousness.

What baffled scientists even more was the question 'who was observing who?' Was it their conscious observation that created the photons to become particles? Or were the photons watching the observer, and behaved like particles when being watched?

Wow! Even modern day physicists have elaborated on these and other discoveries in this field with very mind bending quotes. For instance, N. David Mermin (a solid-state physicist at Cornell University) commented.

[7] *' We now know that the moon is demonstrably not there when nobody looks'.*

Obviously coming to this statement from the fact that the quantum particles acted like waves when no one was watching. And since everything is made up and constructed at base level from quantum particles, it was fair to assume theoretically that the moon wouldn't be there if no one was observing.

Fortunately for the existence of the Universe and the Earth the moon obviously is there, because it was there long before man had evolved onto this planet to even admire it and thoughtfully just make it appear. So here begs the question, if quantum particles only act like particles when they're observed consciously, who was observing the Universe to hold it all together before us?

No one was, because it is the Universe itself that is pure consciousness and it is this pure consciousness that formed the material based Universe to begin with. Matter cannot produce consciousness, but consciousness as scientists have discovered with the double slit experiment, can produce matter.

Consider the modern-day theory of evolution, a theory that cannot logically explain how life suddenly arose, conscious aware life. Now for a moment consider a different theory, my knowing or understanding from my own truth is that consciousness has always been there. Consciousness was there before time and space began, and it is this higher consciousness that manifested our material Universe, or created our Big Bang as we call it, the beginning point.

I choose to see the Big Bang as more of a 'Big Birth'. The birth of our Universe. Just as a child grows, so does our Universe. Not just physically, but also mentally; like human development, the Universe self-learns and gets better. We call this evolution. And at the root of all material manifestations is thought or consciousness.

It is this interconnected omnipotent consciousness that manifested life as we know it. There is no start point to life in this Universe, the Universe is full of life, because the Universe is life, it is life itself, from end to end from the smallest quantum unit to the largest star in the Universe, it is all one and it is all alive.

Consciousness is God, and the Universe is pure consciousness and all is connected. I hope you can begin to see the connection here regarding yourself and your creator. And that in essence, in part you are the creator. There is no delay when we talk to God or the Universal consciousness, the force is omnipotent and intertwined within the fabric of everything, there is no delay between you and the Universal consciousness, God. The phone line has been operational since the day you were born, yet we have been deceived to think it is elsewhere, that God only listens to the anointed chosen few. That God resides in Heaven a place far from here in another realm. That to find God you need to go to a church or a mosque. Do you see now how irrelevant these places are?

These are childlike views at best, and reflect the thinking of the human race from times before modern science began to unfold and discover the true workings of the Universe.

I know it's a lot to take in but no one can deny from this new information that the Universe is so much more intelligently designed than we ever believed, if this doesn't sway opinion over one divine omnipotent force call it God, call it a higher intelligence or just consciousness, then nothing will, because if science ever walked hand in hand with the idea of a Universal all connected force then surely it is now, as the facts speak clearly; we are but a small unique piece of a conscious whole. If subatomic particles are all interconnected and I'm made of the same substance, then I am the Universe and so are you.

Of course, science will never admit openly to a God or God force being responsible for the Universe, instead science will endeavour to try any theory to negate a supernatural existence that acts inside or outside the realms of time and space. We will get to this in a short while, as new theories from Scientists are created in an attempt to deny this undiscoverable force.

There is a paper from the field of physics that tries to explain how matter sprang from the nothingness of the vacuum of space. It is the 'Something from nothing' theory. We mentioned this at the beginning of the book. So, with your new insight and a quick reminder that the vacuum of space is not empty, but instead full of quantum particles and potential energy. This should now help you quickly erase this theory of 'something from nothing'. Especially now that you have some understanding of how the quantum realm works. Everything in the material world is a manifestation from the quantum realm. So, that vacuum full of 'nothing', actually contains the building blocks to new planets, stars and galaxies.

Science as mentioned previously, endeavours for truth and fact; the truth is, how can you quantify this force? Something that exists outside matter, space and time? How can you measure, weigh, calibrate or calculate any way into a mathematical equation that which gives no size to be measured, leaves no trace to be weighed and nothing to be calculated, other than its mark? A divine set of numbers, mathematical impossibilities and other far reaching phenomenon.

Here's an interesting fact quantum physics has discovered, ponder upon this and then draw your own conclusions.

When quantum physicists take two subatomic particles that resonate at exactly the same frequency whatever changes they make to particle one will instantly affect particle two. This may not sound much but this can be achieved over great distances. For example, you could have one particle in a laboratory here somewhere and the other could be put right at the edge of the Universe billions of light years away, and still whatever change we make to particle one, will mirror in particle two, with no delay. Literally instantly. What does this tell us? Well it tells us that despite the light taking billions of years to get here, and that the speed of light is the fastest known speed in the Universe, that somehow these subatomic particles transfer information quicker. This is true, and they definitely do transfer the information faster as they are not restrained by the matter based Universe's restriction of time. It is instant, this is because the subatomic particles that make up you and me have been shown and proven to be able to exist outside the realms of space and time, the information doesn't travel from particle one to particle two as there is no distance to travel. Remember quantum particles do not follow the rules of matter, time and space. If you exist outside the realm of space and time then there is no time to be measured and no distance to travel, it is instantaneous. Proving without doubt that everything is connected. And because particle one resonates at the same frequency as particle two then in essence particle one and two are identical and the same.

This is astonishing and this is how complex yet simple the Universe works, scientists are hoping to use this information to create greater communications over immense distances with the transfer of information being instantaneous.

Anyone that would like to argue still that the subatomic world has no effect on us please consider this. If two identical particles exhibit this connected behaviour over infinite distances, then could this explain the twin phenomenon where one identical twin can get hurt and the other regardless of distance feels the pain? Being identical twins means they resonate at similar frequencies, maybe identical. So, are they behaving like the identical subatomic particles? I think it is certainly interesting when we consider that we now know that we're all interconnected through one Universal consciousness and that we're essentially made up of trillions of these subatomic particles that defy reality and can exist outside the usual matter based confines of time and space.

The truth is that the Universe is bigger and more complex than we could ever imagine, and it truly is a masterpiece that supports life, the Universe we call home is not merely the winning ticket Universe in a possibility of millions of failed Universes. In fact, there is only one Universe that we know to, one Universe created without mistakes, a Universe that has a panoply of life, the vast majority of which we will never ever know about and it is our Universe.

Anyone that may be thinking I'm grasping straws then remember this, science will always attempt to find another solution other than God, and in this case, they would rather have you believe that a billion other universes were created, all from spontaneous creation (even though physically impossible) than accept the overwhelming truth of there only being one known perfect Universe.

For many years science has told us life existed on this planet by pure luck, for example the luck of having water, being the right distance from the Sun, and having the right ingredients for life. This was the common theory, the theory of luck! It sounds quite familiar to the multiverse idea, in that yet again we are lucky to be alive in this one in a billion Universe. Fortunately, anyone awakened enough can see that these 'luck' theories avoid scientists putting their neck out on the block.

Scientists in the past wanted to believe life only existed here by luck because the last thing any educated scholar wanted to do was say that the Universe is full of life, because of the backlash from peers, as the question of extra-terrestrial life has been avoided for decades, most probably due to the early influence of religion, and the idea that we were the only beings in the Universe. However, this is a quickly changing view. Many scientists now believe that the cosmos is full of life. New science is showing that there are literally billions of Earth like planets in our own galaxy. And hence on one, there must be life.

Now we're seeing it again where the 'luck' card is being thrown into the creation of our Universe in an attempt this time to avoid the only real factor that can answer the creation and complexity of our Universe and that is God. You should be able to understand why professional academics would not want to put theories forward of God without any hard evidence, however there are a number of scientists coming forward now saying that the 'God force' or God is the missing factor that joins all the dots regarding our existence.

Sadly, as we know most scientists will put forward godless theories without any evidence at all, and ultimately any theory without a creator can only point to an accidental creation. We know that nothing hasn't ever created anything, it is just impossible. And yet any story that omits a creator is clearly stating that nothing did in fact create this splendid Universe in which we live, a Universe so complex it is genius.

The evidence of a higher force or God is everywhere in our Universe, there is clear proof of coding systems and design paradigms as mentioned previously.

Another interesting link we can make between the paranormal and the subatomic world is within the realm of clairvoyance or any other spiritual work. As everything is connected universally through consciousness and all is one, does this explain how a sitter can have information extracted from the atmosphere, regarding loved ones they have lost by a medium or clairvoyant etc. Is the clairvoyant really talking to the dead? Or has the clairvoyant somehow unknowing to themselves managed to open up that particular information from the Universal consciousness? The Universal consciousness will naturally contain all the information the Universe has collected from the dawn of time until now, and beyond. Because everything is connected the clairvoyant doesn't actually draw the information out, rather the clairvoyant already holds the information in their own collective consciousness? As their own consciousness is still part of the Universal consciousness. It is an interesting question, and regardless of the answer it is certainly fair to say that all the old paranormal riddles that past science couldn't answer with the matter based model can now be questioned again with quantum physics, we've already questioned the twin phenomenon and clairvoyance, and found reasonable possible answers, even one of the biggest questions of all can be answered using this new quantum based model of our Universe, 'how was the great pyramid constructed?'

      Despite the historians best attempts it seems difficult to believe that each multi-ton block was dragged and lifted, you could not get enough men around a 20-ton block to lift it let alone a 70-ton block, but what if you changed the vibration of the subatomic particles that manifest the material block. Like the unseen forces at work when we spoke of the crystal wine glass and how a certain frequency makes the particles move quicker, could the same principle have been employed on the stones making them lighter and easier to lift? Or maybe even levitated the stones completely? It all sounds crazy yet is all possible with this new information. Rumours went around recently of a group of scientists at a University that had levitated an object from one side of the room to the other using frequency. The objects were only small; screws, bolts etc. But clearly the implications are huge.

The following quote comes from an online article regarding levitating small objects. The research is being conducted at Tokyo University. Clearly, we're entering a whole new age of technology.

8. *"What the Tokyo University team has done is build upon the idea, by combining soundwaves in three dimensions. The video shows not just tiny little plastic balls being levitated and controlled, but also resistors, LEDs, screws, bolts and other small items."*

An interesting piece of information is that the Universe is essentially made up of three energies these are matter (manifestation of consciousness), which constitutes to 5% which is everything we can see in the known Universe, from the world around us, to the planets, stars and galaxies. Right up to the very edge of what is.

Then there is dark matter or antimatter which makes up 27% (the space between space) that holds it all together and dark energy. Dark energy makes up some 67% of our Universe and is thought to be responsible for the Universes expansion and yet it is not made up of the same stuff the Universe is, so what is it? It is all around us yet scientists cannot fathom out what it is, here is a thought, and it's only a thought because I am certainly no theoretical physicist, but could the dark energy be the place where other dimensions exist? Is it where the afterlife is? It is there all around us yet it is not made up of the same stuff, so what could it be? It is certainly very interesting. Or is it the source of pure consciousness and our creator itself? It's compelling to think that the material part of the Universe only contributes to 5% of the known Universe.

So this is the quantum Universe that you are a part of, we won't discuss any more because a thousand books could be wrote on quantum physics, I have merely mentioned this subject as it shows how our Universe truly works, it is not a vast empty space of nothingness at all, but rather, one living conscious entity and we're all a part of it, we are not some inert creatures just roaming around looking for something to do, we are part of something magnificent, something spectacular and something divine.

Can we say with scientific evidence and with reasonable knowing that the Universe is all connected, with each part being as significant as the whole? Yes.

Is it fair to say with scientific evidence that we're merely not just matter based beings, but rather conscious beings, constructed from subatomic particles, consciousness holding things together and a part of one Universal consciousness? Yes.

And finally, can we now say with knowing that there is an underlying connected energy that connects each and every one of us, that is found here and stretches to the edge of our Universe and the space in between that brings life throughout its realm? Yes.

Can we call this force God? That is for you to decide my friend.

If we reflect back to the beginning chapters we discussed together the idea of social conditioning and media conditioning and its effects on our self, and how it affects our 'true self', and remember earlier how we discussed Jesus having his own truth, that was different to Muhammed and to Buddha's own truth.

Although it may be very apparent what my opinion is, the last thing I want you the reader to do is merely take it as fact. I'm hoping that as the reader you open yourself up, release former content and beliefs and then look with all your heart and every inch of your being at what you see in the Universe around you, question the world around you and not just regurgitate dogmatic views, but rather discover your own place, identity and own unique view.

Truth is a journey with no fixed path, this is where religion fails, you do not become spiritually awakened from learning about God from an ancient book, but rather we become awakened through the experience of life, every day in every way. Living our own unique path. It is a personal experience between your consciousness and the consciousness of God, but remember there is no real separation between the two. As we are the manifestation of Gods consciousness.

And from this standpoint and perspective you should hopefully begin to discover your own Universal truths. Truths that when you discover them they empower you, truths that pull you away from the dogmatic patterns of thought unique to our own societies viewpoint.

With this information in mind you should now start to realise that you haven't been born to merely just survive and then die, you were born with a purpose, a gift, a talent, something that maybe you do every day, maybe something that you haven't done in a while, but it was this universal gift that has always been nagging away at you that was meant to be your purpose, your frequency and the doorway back to your 'true self', strong and empowered in the knowing that you have a purpose.

That nagging voice in the back of your head that speaks so quietly but persists endlessly, is your 'true self' screaming at you to make the necessary changes. Now we understand a little of how the Universe works and continuously communicates with itself, we should start to see how simple it should be to hear your calling.

Chapter 8

Be The Change.

Just as we were created by the Universe, and are of the Universe, it seems our greatest gift of all is our own opportunity to create a better world, not just for ourselves but also for the world in general. We the created, from billions of years of conscious evolution of our Universe have the power to create, and this is our most unappreciated gift of all. It is we alone and not through guidance, that need to become the change we wish to see in the world. We the people need to stand up for what is right, if we know for example that someone is doing something that is truly wrong, then I beg you to be the karma the world needs and say or do something.

As people, we often seek shelter and hide from trouble, and what has this done for society? It has not done much. We as people should step in and point out that what they're doing is wrong, I began doing this a few years ago, and if I'm honest it feels really good. I've questioned adults that I have seen be approached by children to buy them cigarettes, and have purchased them, knowing the child is not old enough. I've asked them what they think they are doing? And 'how would they feel if someone did that for their children?'

I've stopped my car when I have seen someone struggling and asked if they were ok? I run a tattoo studio and once whilst tattooing, a customer informed me that he had his gas cut off from his house and had not had a hot shower for a long time and I could see this. As soon as the tattoo was finished I informed him that there was a shower upstairs with hot running water and that he was free to use it if he so wished. He went home and returned about half hour later with his towel and took me up on my simple offer.

It is these small offerings that will truly help the world which is so desperate for change. I remember after he had the shower having a chat with him, I thought it appropriate to mention that maybe getting the tattoo should have come second to paying his gas bill.

If you're thinking that this lifestyle of being the positive change will not benefit you then please take a moment and see just how violent and self-centred society has become. The world would truly be a different place if the greater majority adopted this way of living life. It is disappointing that a lot of people from this would automatically get their backs up and say 'why should I bother if they don't?' The answer...this is our only way of making the world better. For you, your family and future generations.

The ever increasing 'walk on by' attitude is decaying social conduct and social moral. People are inherently good, some just need to be shown the right way. What is so evident by our own nature is that if the leaders amongst us took this approach to life, then the masses that seek to only follow would comply without effort. Just a quick note, when I say leaders I do not mean the leaders of nations although that would be great. The world leaders however are merely just a few. There are leaders that walk amongst us every day, you may be one. Leaders that people look up to, leaders within small communities that do not fully understand the influence they may have. The people that within small communities, the other local people look up to. You could be a local sports role model, a teacher, a parent, you could be anyone. You could even be the local tough guy. People are watching, always. Our examples lead others. Each town has these people, and these people can influence on a level more positively than any preaching done within the confines of a religious building. The world changers lead, and lead by example without fear. They live with compassion, with love and with a knowing that they are of a greater calling and of a greater more important existence.

Society should always punish any criminal lawfully as this is the correct procedure, but how many times does the law system fall drastically short? How many criminals are free? How many elderly people get robbed and beaten? And how many children are getting abused? We need change. And most of all we need to stop living in a fear driven mindset. Remember the water buffalo and our discussion on the brutality of life? Well remember just how easy we have it.

We have the power to literally change our own lives. Our own thoughts and perception will decide whether we have a scared existence or whether we have a rich and free one.

Just think for a moment and consider the two outlooks towards life. There's outlook one, the negative outlook. An outlook that looks elsewhere for blame, an outlook that is selfish, an outlook obsessed with material gain, an outlook blind to the wondrous world around them, a world from which they have evolved through years of evolution, and yet a magnificent world that is hidden from them because of the blindness of their material goals, and material conditioning.

Then of course we have the opposite, we have an outlook of optimism, one of knowing and understanding, one where we allow our minds to open up fully to the world and Universe around us. An outlook where even the greatest challenges life throws at us, are seen as just that, challenges. A standpoint empowered by the understanding of being free, free from fear, and with this in my mind there is nothing we cannot achieve.

    Once the bonds and the ties that confine us to three-dimensional thinking are gone, we begin to open up and begin to see the Universe in a different light, the restraints of other people's mindsets start to become broken, and then when the world around you becomes quiet, something within you opens up, but only once the noise stops. I truly believe that everyone has this ability. Too many of the ancient books speak of prophets, messiahs etc. I truly do not doubt the integrity of any of them that have come before us. But we must remember this, by separating these individuals and placing them on pedestals we denounce our own divine connection. Your first step to achieving truth is accepting the ultimate truth. You are a child of the Universal consciousness and you are as important and as connected to the energy of everything as these individuals are. It is the path they walked that is different. And as mentioned from my own experience, the journey that you can also choose to take. Both inwardly seeking truth of self, and outwardly seeking truth of the Universe (the world around you).

    Once these steps are taken you will soon discover a conversation between yourself and the consciousness of the Universe, God begins. It has actually always been going on. Life and all of its wonderful distractions slowly make the conversation go quiet. Once you learn to quieten the noise of the world the conversation will begin to be heard again. My conversation began consciously many years ago.

Chapter 9

Connecting With The Universal Consciousness.

There are states of mind we exhibit as humans. I'm no Psychologist so please try and follow me. We seem to display different levels of awareness regarding our own consciousness. Most of the world walks around in a haze not consciously aware of their current actions, and we are all guilty of it; some are a guiltier than others. For instance, I have seen on numerous occasions people hold a door open for a stranger and the stranger just walk through the door without acknowledging the kind gesture and saying thank you. It can be a tedious path 'being the change'.

I have seen people throw rubbish on the floor in the street when there has been a bin only yards away from them. In most cases if you actually took the time to stop one of these people and point out that there was a bin only yards away then most would be embarrassed and probably say sorry and then attempt to put right what they had done wrong.

Yes, along the way you will inevitably meet someone that might just tell you unpolitely to go away. However, most would stop and apologise. So why does this happen? What makes a person that is clearly competent seem rude, unthankful or just 'away with the fairies?' You will begin to notice this when you begin to live as a more 'consciously awake' person. When you start living more aware

It is quite simple why most seem rude, unthankful or 'away with the fairies'. Most people are unaware of the current moment when they are engaged in modern day living with all its hurrying about. With the fast-paced life, we live we often forget about the 'moment' and can be normally found focusing on tomorrow's issues, even next weeks! You may be hurrying about thinking about what you did yesterday, maybe stressing about an argument with the family or an appointment you missed earlier today. All these non-productive thoughts pull the focus of your consciousness away from the current world, from the current moment. And quickly an attitude of living in your own head develops.

This is not healthy, let's quickly recap on the beginning of this chapter and what we said about people being next to a bin and yet still throwing their rubbish on the floor and not even noticing the bin. If in this mind state we struggle, and miss in our world such a simple object like a bin, then what else are we missing? What other aspects of life are we mindlessly walking past?

A conscious mind needs to be developed, a mind alert enough to stay fixed in the 'now', in the present situation. Many use meditations to achieve such a state of awareness, however quite simply being aware of it is the first step. Initially begin by monitoring your thoughts, see how often your mind will try to distract you. It takes time to develop, but in time you will begin to retrain what your mind is accustomed to, and develop a mind less hectic and more focused. A mind that is in the 'now'.

I am very blessed in my job because I have to stay in a high state of awareness. My mind is not allowed to drift, if my mind slips away somebody receives a bad tattoo. Therefore now, and developed over time I find myself readily aware and in the 'now'.

Not only will you see more and take in more of the world around you but you will also begin to open up.

Once the noise of the outside world grows quiet, an inner journey seems to begin and you become open to the Universal consciousness, God. God can't leave you an email or a post-it note. The message is for you, your path, your purpose and your destiny. If you can't focus your mind and consciousness into the 'now', then how will you ever hear your calling?

The ancient Hindus believed all could be known through meditation. All the answers that could not be found externally could be answered internally, simply by quietening the world around them. Meditation is a wonderful part of life to develop but, and it is a significant 'but', how many people have the time to sit and meditate every day for 30 mins or more? In today's fast paced life, we simply do not get the free time to meditate, well not in the conventional manner of sitting in the lotus position for long periods of time. That does not mean a state of total awareness similar to that achieved through meditation cannot be achieved without meditation. Meditation itself, in its name alone will evoke images in your mind of what you presume meditation is, or how you 'should' sit whilst doing it. This is purely preconditioning from media sources. A state of awareness that is in the 'now', is how our consciousness works in its true natural state, free from fear and thoughts of tomorrow or yesterday. Names such as meditation and set procedures simply solidify actions that were once natural and fluid, resulting in a world where people ask 'to be taught' or ask 'to be shown' how to meditate. Another sad example of how we are taught to seek externally that which is truly known internally.

We discussed a few chapters ago about how the connection between you and the Universal consciousness is constant and forever. Simply keep your mind clear and in the now. You will at times slip into old ways but in time the new way will replace the old patterns. It is your design to live in the now, it is purely modern day living that has changed this part of your nature. To meditate without meditation is easy, so simple that you can begin right now. Learn to monitor your thoughts as they unfold, see how many times your mind will attempt to pull you away from your current actions. Stay strong and persist in your mindset of a consciousness that is aware and in the now. The changes your life will receive over such a short period of time will be massive if these simple changes are made.

 Consciously make the change to wake up from your slumber. No more living by routine like a programmed robot. No more drifting out of reality to hide from the present, no more walking around having little effect on the world.

 Instead awaken from your sleep and seize every moment, be aware of your actions and positively make the world a better place; even the smallest 'thank you' can lighten up someone's dark day. No more hectic behaviour fuelled by a hectic mind, instead positive results driven from an aware mind. Be 'fully aware', and deal with things as they come and then put them aside both in life and in your mind. This is essential and the key to stress free living. Too many people put of till tomorrow what should be done today. When a hurdle arrives deal with it. It will not always be achievable, and the hurdle may be too high, but accepting this truth and trying for a new approach is far more productive than simply hoping it will go away. Leaving the problem in the back of your mind and not dealing with it actually keeps your mind occupied with the problems that it simply does not need. This is the noise of the outside world. You have a choice on how much you are interrupted on your true-life path by how much time you waste on such trivial tasks.

Free yourself and open up to living the way the Universe intended you to. The benefits will be massive, as your actions affect your family, your career, your home, your friends and even your health. All aspects of your life will benefit from this simple shift of consciousness. Try and have times of quiet and solitude. A quiet mind is a peaceful mind. The greatest level you can achieve in this state is what some refer to as 'mindfulness'. A mind that is so in the 'now', that it is a mind full of nothing (other than the surrounding senses at that time). If you can achieve this, you will master your life on every level. This is achieved because you will be in total control of all your actions, from the food you put in your mouth to how you behave around your children. You may even find yourself acting in new ways towards all aspects of your life. An unconditioned mind truly is a creative mind.

I need you to trust in what I am going to share with you in the next chapter. It is the truth and please believe me I have explored every possible logical route to explain the phenomenon I still see every day. It is truly magnificent and feeling truly blessed I have wrote this book in an attempt to share my experience. I have shared my own discoveries, and shared my thoughts for discussion. My main aim is to open up as many people as I possibly can to a phenomenon that has changed my whole outlook to every aspect of my entire life. I listened, and this is me, 'being the change'. It really is that simple.

You never know you may also begin to experience things not so explainable. Little synchronicities you never noticed before in your sleepy state. I'd been receiving a calling card for years and had never even noticed until one day...

Chapter 10

The 33 And 333 Phenomenon.

Have you ever been thrust awake out of bed in the middle of the night? If you have, have you ever picked your phone up to check the time? Well most of us have or even woke up to look at the bedside clock to check the time? How many of you have ever seen the time and began to become increasingly terrified at its persistence to grab your attention? I'm guessing not many are relating to this now. Please as crazy and as far out as this may sound I ask you to remain open minded.

Around 6 years ago, I began waking up at 3:33am every morning, not 3:32am or 3:34am, but specifically 3:33am. I even tried to trick myself by adjusting the clocks in the house so that all were out of sync in an attempt to stop the phenomenon, just in case my subconscious brain had developed some set synchronicity that I was not aware of. However, despite all my clocks having no continuity I kept seeing 3:33, and it was increasing to all clocks. The clock in my car, at home and at my studio including the CCTV monitor. To say that it was beginning to unnerve me was an understatement.

Then to make matters even more spookier I began seeing 333 and 33 all around me in my daily life, from number plates, to digital displays on home gadgets, the thermostat, laptop, oven etc. I don't just mean that I literally just saw these numbers, as there's nothing really strange about that. What I mean is, I would be deep into a video on the internet and my eyes for no reason at all would be drawn away from the screen, to look up and see a car driving past my window with the registration containing 333, or I would be tattooing away and glance up at my monitor and notice it displaying 2:33pm and 3 seconds.

I could calculate mathematically the chance of seeing 33 on the clock in minutes, that was simple. It was a 1 in a 60 chance, but I couldn't begin to comprehend the probability of looking up at my monitor and seeing 33 minutes and 3 seconds. I would be driving my car, glance down and notice that the mileage would have 333 somewhere dominant in its configuration.

All these times that I see the number I am truly not knowingly looking for it, it seems as though something deeper within myself is connected and very aware of it, and taking my attention towards it at every opportunity.

Anyway, with this fear of the unknown starting to build, I did what any responsible adult would do at this time, and I sat down and googled the meaning of 333. I say this with a hint of humour, but most of us have done this as a first port of call for information.

There was not much to be found initially for myself, just little scraps here and there, but over time and at different points of discovery the truth started to be revealed.

What came back astounded me. It seems all through religion and secret societies, the number 3, 33 and 333 turns up. I will share now what I have learned about this phenomenon, and at the end give you some crazy truths about myself that I have discovered since I learned how to listen.

The number 3 sits on its own as the only real 'true' number, and so was given the title of 'Truth' by many ancient cultures. This initially compelled me because truth was something I had always been obsessed with from an early age. It is given this title as the number 3 is the only number that is the sum of its preceding numbers, 1+2=3. No other number does this, sit and try it. Let's take the number 4 for instance, 1,2,3,4 1+2+3+4=10 and not 4. Try it with any number, it only happens with the number 3.

So, the number three has always been synonymous with truth. You can see it displayed yet hidden in ancient symbols of many cultures. I will show a few pics later in the chapter that will demonstrate what I mean. Also, these numbers 3, 33 and 333 seem to occur readily within religion. What is interesting like I previously mentioned is that I am not alone in this phenomenon, there are many worldwide that are also experiencing it, some are just on the early stages of their development, some may experience a 'Messiah' complex believing that they are somehow better than others because they are experiencing and engaging with the Universe in a different way to before. I can remember feeling like this at the beginning. It is hard for any human mind not to feel incredibly special when the truth regarding that 'what is' becomes revealed through the experience of life. Sadly, this is ego and as we know, ego is no good.

In the first chapter I described how if I could bottle the feelings that I have, I would be a billionaire. This is no weak statement; the sense of warmth, love and inner happiness I feel when I get a revelation is beyond measure.

If you are experiencing this phenomenon, then please embrace it and take it as a calling card for you. Be thankful and start being led by God the Universal consciousness, and accept the truth. If you're experiencing this phenomenon then you know the first truth already, God exists, and readily and easily communicates through the Universal consciousness, as God is the Universal consciousness.

I cannot emphasise enough that I follow no religion, but I must at this point add that I do have at home a variety of religious books from different cultures and beliefs. How can you try and understand something without reading into it?

History is filled with wars based on religion and difference of opinions regarding the 'truth' and the 'one true god'. Anyone awakened enough quickly realises how disgusting this behaviour is. To add to this the image of God that was created in these books is wrong, God is no man, God doesn't sit on a cloud, looking down angry at us handing out punishment. I knew this implicitly because of my own divine experience that was unfolding before me.

I felt pure love from my experience, and yet I don't go to church, and do not follow any set doctrines. I do talk to God every day, many times, I don't feel a man's presence watching over me, I feel an energy, a harmony, a love for all.

From my path or journey the true essence of 33 or 333 for myself is threefold. I will touch upon this now and go into more depth in the final chapter.

The first overwhelming truth is that God exists. This profound truth was shown to me in a way that was truly just for me. Your confirmation may have come already in another form. The Universal consciousness knows us inside out, hence it knows already what we need to be shown when we just ask. My link was synchronicity, science and discovering my 'true self'. My synchronicity came in the form of the 3's. Along my journey, I have since discovered that the higher force of the Universe has repeatedly used the symbol that we call 'three' in all cultures to convey truth, and used this as a clear symbol of communication as in my own unique case.

The second is the understanding of we and the importance of we. A singular conscious force manifested into reality by a higher consciousness, God. I am not important. What is important is we, and the way we choose to live our lives to help the many. We are all of the Universe, and we are all created from the same force. Our lives are different and our goals are different, and our truths are our own. Yet it all functions as one.

Think of our Universe as a whole, that whole functions on many levels, on levels we will never comprehend, just think back to what we have learned together whilst reading this text, and just how little we still understand. Or think of the workings of a clock, all parts perform different tasks that ultimately make the whole work. Would the clock work if every part was the second hand? Of course not.

The essence of all of this is not to judge. Once we begin to realise that our goals and sometimes our ideals are different, we can stop judging others when we do not understand them. Simply stated if you believe in the Universal consciousness, God and the genius of nature, then who are we, who are of little understanding, to judge? The problem with most is that they try to understand everything and why things happen, the truth is that the Universe is beyond our full comprehension, however once you begin to embrace that you are connected and a part of a higher force then you will begin to understand your own existence, and hopefully one day look back and finally understand God's plan that was set out for you and just you alone.

The third and final lesson my experience has conveyed to me is that the greatest task is to accept the power and importance of self and the effect we have on the world; as we are in our own way creators. Once this role is accepted, learn to know oneself. Journey inwards, begin to understand your fears, learn your 'true self' from your ego, only by knowing yourself can you change yourself, and only by changing and changing for the better will we ever change the world. This is God's creation reflected in you, the greatest gift we all have, yet few choose to embrace it. How scary would it be to never blame anyone else for our own mistakes, but to instead look inward and learn what we did wrong? Few will be strong enough to choose this path, and the many will still choose to make decisions and then when things do not go there way sit and choose to blame others. It is an easy path living this way, yet unfortunate in so many ways. The biggest loss is spending a lifetime with someone and never truly knowing them, that person being you. In the final chapter, we shall discuss these three truths further and in a lot more detail.

      Some people that experience this phenomenon of seeing repeating patterns in numbers may as mentioned already begin to develop a messiah complex, which again places the emphasis on 'I', and a psychology of them being better than others. You should realise the importance of self, we are all God, just in miniature version, but no one is better or more special than anyone else, as we're all given this gift from birth.

      You are not in competion with the next person...you are only competing against yourself, to simply be a better version in every way and every day.

      The Universe has conversed with humanity forever, and one day we will die and the conversation continues elsewhere.

      So, find your own truth, love one another and listen, switch off all the noise and listen, our creator has spoken to you from the moment you arrived here, your dreams your goals your ambitions, you have just forgotten how to truly listen.

This experience I'm having can be beautifully demonstrated in this verse from the Bible. By no means am I suddenly endorsing Christianity as I would not endorse any religion nor negate any religion, we discussed religion in great detail earlier, however like I said the 333 phenomenon is not new, and not confined to just Christianity and this is a great beginning to demonstrate synchronicity between this number and a conversation with the Universe or God.

Along my path, I stumbled accidentally upon this next verse from the New Testament and the Book of Jeremiah. Like I said earlier these little insights came long after I began seeing the numbers. The 333 was present again in this experience and naturally it was the 333 that caught my attention.

In Jeremiah 33:3 of the King James Bible it says
'Call unto me, and I will answer thee, and show you great and mighty things which thou knowest not'.

This passage struck me like a bolt of lightning. It lays out in one sentence the journey I have been on, a journey of discovery and truth regarding our place in the big scheme of things. Basically, this passage is saying believe and call unto God, and things that are not known will be revealed.

Please remember I only discovered this passage a year ago, yet it's clearly saying just ask.

Again, in another text the 333 popped up again, and yes it was purely by chance. In the Hindu religion within the Yoga Sutra 3:33 it states

'Through keenly developed intuition everything can be known'.

Is this not saying the same thing again? Here we have two separate religions, two religions of different time scales, geographically miles apart regarding their own origins, and yet not only are both saying the same thing, but both have the number 333 attached to them. This is no coincidence, this is the synchronicity of the Universe, this is God the Universal consciousness at work.

Even though the Yoga Sutra uses the term intuition rather than God, it is still saying the same thing. What is intuition? Intuition is gut instinct, going with feelings rather than thought, intuition is never thought. A developed intuition is an awakened, chain free consciousness. And what is pure consciousness? We now know consciousness is God.

Here are a few examples within religion where the image of a number 3 is being used, sometimes, well most times not noticed and passed off for something else entirely. The first example is the Om. Take a look at the symbol below and tell me that the symbol on the left is not a number 3.

Figure 13. The Om

It certainly is drawn that way, and the Om is one of the most widely known symbols of spirituality. The Om symbol design is a symbolic representation of the various parts of the psyche. An inner dimensional map of the various compartments of human consciousness and the relationship each has to the divine within. Sound familiar?

A great example of this symbol being hidden in plain sight is within the religion of Islam. Take a look at the Islamic symbol for God. What struck me straight away was that the symbol for God only needed a 90-degree counter-clockwise rotation and 33 was clearly visible.

الله

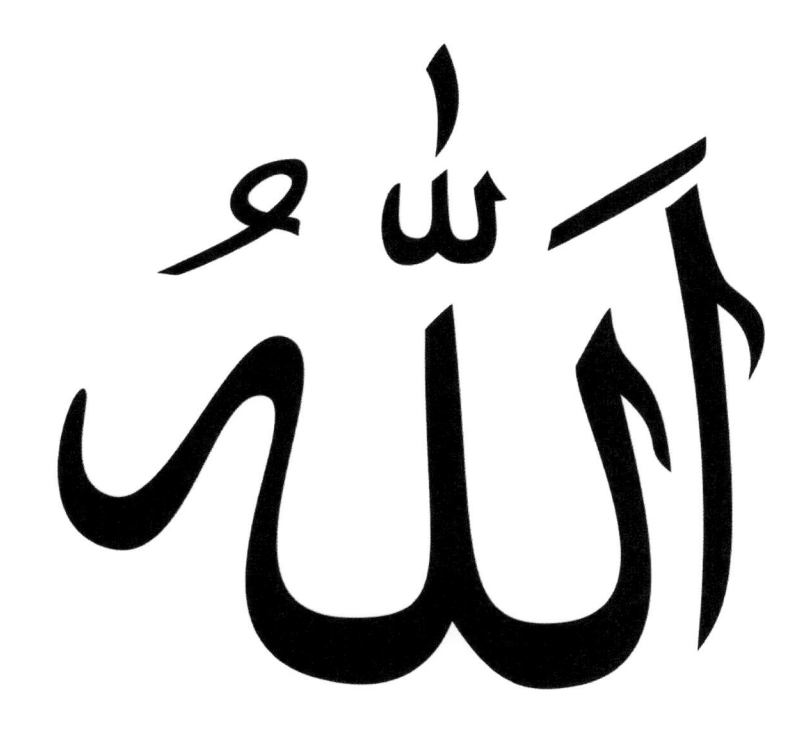

Figure 14. Islamic symbol for God.

    For a moment, I thought I was grasping straws until something compelled me to search the number 3 in Arabic. Below is a clock from Cairo train station, notice the number 3.

Figure 15. Arabic numerals on clock face.

There it was clear as you like, no need for rotation. The Arabic way of writing a number 3 was exactly the same as the symbol on the Islamic banner for God. And I was clearly seeing a 33.

It seems the number 3 is used quite a lot. In Pagan worship, all things done are done to the power of three. In Christianity, there is the holy trinity, the Father, the Son and the Holy spirit. Jesus Christ who was given the title of truth died aged 33. 3 is the number of the resurrection as after 3 days and 3 nights Jesus was resurrected again. In the book of Revelations, we see several references to destruction and judgement where 1/3 is destroyed. 1/3 = 33.33333%.

There are according to the Hindu texts 333 million variations of Brahma. A lot of people literally believe that the Hindu faith has 333 million different gods, however a lot of evidence points to this being a misinterpretation of the truth. In Hinduism, they believe in one creator, Brahma. The 333 million gods come from

152

the belief that this was the population of the planet when the Hindu texts were written. And the 333 million gods refer to the 333 million manifestations of God, because each individual has their own relationship with God, and as we're all different, God's manifestation from our own unique perspective is reflected by this.

Originally this little section was not included but it seems right up until the very end the Universe still has so much to show regarding this number. We have already viewed this image but let's now take a closer look.

Figure 16. Lord Shiva

I cannot believe that I was saved this little gem for last. Clearly on the centre of Shivas head is a 33. Notice that it mirrors on the third eye. Interestingly Shiva is part of a Trimurti, three Hindu Gods, including Brahma, Vishnu and Shiva. I do not believe it any coincidence that Shiva, the God of destruction and creation clearly wears the marking of 33. This is exactly what we are discussing in this book. The destruction of the ego to bring forward into existence the 'true self'. The destruction of the old reality replaced with a new one.

The realisation of the 'self' as a creator.

On the next image, we see Brahma the Hindu God, notice how 333 is displayed here figuratively, 3 heads, 3 limbs on one side (2 arms and a leg) and 3 limbs on the other.

Figure 17. Brahma statue.

In freemasonry, the 33rd order is the highest order, and these are meant to know the secrets of everything, being given the title 'Illuminated'.

In Buddhism, most acts are performed 3 times as offerings to the 3 jewels, the Buddha, Dharma and

Sangha. When one bows at a Buddhist shrine one always makes 3 prostrations, at the same time offering three sticks of incense. If you made a ceremonial procession around a tomb it would also be done 3 times.

In the Star of David, the symbol is constructed from two triangles, here again we see a 33 in relation to the three-sided triangle overlapping a three-sided triangle.

Figure 18 Star of David.

And finally, we see the 33 displayed in the Sikh religion symbiology of the Khanda.

Figure 19 The Khanda.

On the previous page, we saw the Sikh symbol. It is made up of 3 separate weapons. One double edged sword, two single-edged swords and a circle. What is interesting to note here is the 33 represented by 3 points up and 3 down.

Hopefully you can understand now you've seen a little of what I have seen and noticed. The fact that the Universe isn't quite the inert, non-interactive evolved space dust that we've been led to believe. In fact, even though it is evolved space dust, we now understand that behind the material evolution and development of the Universe there has always been an underlying consciousness, growing and evolving alongside it. Things aren't as inert as it seems, the actual reality is quite the opposite.

If you are still not sold on the 333 phenomena, then see if this changes your mind. I'm sat here writing this penultimate chapter during my summer holiday. It's been a year and a half since the last time I referenced what I was doing personally at the time of writing. Intriguingly enough, it seems I only ever get chance to write this book whilst on my holiday breaks from work.

This is purely because of how busy my studio is, like I said earlier I'm a Fine Art Tattooist and blessed to have a full diary weeks in advance. This shift in my personal life came when I began to consciously manifest what I wanted my life or reality to be. I mention my job just so that you understand truthfully that I have sacrificed so much personal time to get this information to you.

I could have quite easily just accepted what I have experienced and kept all this information to myself, or just shared it with my close family and friends. I am very happy and content in my career and I certainly do not intend to develop a career as a writer, I have never enjoyed writing (yet I have thoroughly enjoyed the journey of writing this book). I have an array of hobbies already, from my Art (which includes oil painting), reading non-fiction, working in my garden and home; which I love dearly. I really love my garden, honestly, I can't emphasise just how much, as it is here that I see God's creation at work through the manifestation of my action every day, as I do when I create some beautiful piece of art on a client's skin.

I play the piano, the guitar and alongside all of this train 6 days a week at the gym and run my own limited company, so you can imagine how busy with work I get with just dealing with the day to day chores of running a business. All this mentioned is true, so please try to see that this book, and this message is conveyed to you from a truly selfless perspective.

I was about to share with you the strange connections to 3, 33, and 333 that I have. These dots joined way down the road of my individual path and journey. I guess they answered all of my doubts regarding at the time the phenomenon I was witnessing.

Only last week when we arrived at our hotel we were given the key to room 332. Naturally I couldn't understand why I had been situated next to room 333 and not placed in it. We hadn't requested any particular room number prior to booking, so it was still a bit of a shock anyway. Once the initial laughing and conversation about how we were situated next door to room 333 was over we carried on about our business of getting unpacked.

Later that day I was sat on the balcony and my partner had walked by downstairs and looked up and waved at me. On her arrival back to the room she laughed and said, "Do you realise when you look up our room is exactly 3 floors up and is situated 3rd balcony from the end?". I had not taken the time to look, but when I went down and looked myself it was true, and naturally filled me again with happiness, that the higher force in the Universe was and is still clearly working alongside me.

Only last night I was sat in hotel our room, it was around 12am and my son was watching the movie, Matrix Revolutions. I was considering what was going to be included in this chapter, even considering whether this chapter was even appropriate because the whole number experience was purely a personal one. As I was sitting in contemplation I heard from the T.V. Morpheus (a main character) say, "When I see three objectives, three captains, three ships, I see providence, I see purpose. I believe it our fate to be here, it is our destiny. I believe this night holds for each and every one of us, the very meaning of our lives". There was no doubt that this message was for me, the synchronicity and relevance of the 333 was truly obvious. So, that was that then, the

Universe had clearly spoken, God had the plan, I was writing this chapter!

My conditioning early on had eradicated any following of a belief system from my life. Now I accept and love all that have come before me and walked their path to truth. Buddha, Jesus, Ghandi, Krishnamurti I truly love them all, and despite what the followers may believe and say, I have no doubt that all these guys would have sat down together peacefully and got along. When you find peace within, you find peace outwardly also.

The insight these great men had during their lifetime enabled them to walk with power and peace, it is only those that have followed in their names that have created distaste and judgement, those who have followed and twisted God's work for their own benefit, or for the benefit of their so-called people.

Another strange coincidence is that some internet pages call 33 or 333 the 'Christ consciousness'. And describe the 333 phenomena as walking with the 'ascended masters' (Jesus, Buddha, Krishna, Gandhi). These master numbers are as some spiritual sites describe, 111, 222 and 333, and these numbers have had massive significance in ancient cultures and societies.

Right, I will finally share my own connections to this number anomaly, other than seeing the 33, and 333 everywhere it seems I had also had the number ingrained in me from birth.

Firstly, I have two older brothers, which means I was the 3rd born of 3 boys from my Mother. I have no sisters.

There is the first connection, not much of one I suppose anyone could argue purely coincidental, it is the second connection that is a little freaky. This insight came to someone else at the strangest of times. In fact, I received the phone call from the friend in the middle of the night, they were excited to say the least and couldn't wait to share what they had had revealed to them.

  Let me add at this point that my two older brothers were given very normal and commonly used names. My eldest brother is called Craig, and my other brother is called David. My mother thinking out of the box for her third child decided on calling me Wade. A forename not heard of here in England when I was growing up. Now 41 years later you do tend to hear this name a little more, back in the late 70's early 80's it was unheard of here in England, and with my unusual name in hand I received the usual childhood taunts and bullying associated with being different.

  I can remember one of the songs the kids used to sing to me and now I'm older I do find it funny, but things are different when you're younger. 'Wade, Wade with a bucket and spade' resounded around the school playground for years in infant school.

  I can remember sitting in class and wishing that my name was Paul, something normal and not this strange alien name I had been given. As I got older I embraced my name, I love being different. Anyway, the connection to 33...

  The friend that called me during the night had woken from a dream. I had shared my experience with them regarding the strange number phenomenon over a loose conversation one day. Anyway, it was the middle of the night and the phone rang. "Hello mate", I answered the phone with bleary eyes and a half-awake mind, "what's up?". My friend couldn't get this of his chest quick enough, "Your name, your name equals 33", was the excited response from down the line. My mind quickly woke up as I was intrigued to know what they meant. My friend continued, "I was asleep, and I had a dream, and in the dream it said Wade equals 33, so I did what you showed me with Amen and how that equals 33. If a=1 and b=2 and c=3 etc. (Amen =33 a=1, m=13, e=5, n=14 1+13+14+5=33), well Wade also equals 33!". "Are you sure?" I quickly replied, "Yes, yes check it out"! Of course, excitedly and now wide awake I quickly did the math and my friend was right.

W=23, a=1, d=4, and e=5. 23+1+4+5=33!

It seems that the Universe had plans all along regarding my path, and this was just another divine confirmation showing me again that things seem to be orchestrated by a bigger force, that force being God.

It seems I was also born under master numbers. The ancients refer to the master numbers being 111, 222, 333. All having different meanings. My birth date 22/2/1975. If you add the sum of the 1975, 1+9+7+5 it also equals 22. So, 22,2, 1+9+7+5=22, becomes 22,2,22. Another strange anomaly regarding my existence.

I've now shared with you a big part of my journey. Some will relate to some of the things that I have said, naturally others will not. As I mentioned at the very beginning of this book, this is no authority. It is simply a sharing of my own particular journey. What you do with this information is purely for you to decide and no one else. Now that I have shared my own journey, I will now share with you the reader what I have been taught along the way.

Chapter 11

The Final Chapter

The Revelation.

So, it seems from before I was born the Universal consciousness, God had a plan, from my moment of birth, to my placement alongside my brothers to my name, the 33, 333 phenomena were already playing out.

I forgot to mention in the last chapter that I also live at house number 3, in a road name that has 3 letters. Everything discovered after I started noticing the numbers. This string of events in itself reveals and confirms the first truth, at least for myself anyway.

God truly exists. There is no doubt. My experience is an inner one, it cannot be quantified, or theoretically explained, it is what it is. My experience has shown me on a spiritual level, that there is no doubt to there being bigger forces at work in this, our known Universe.

Scientifically, there can be no doubt that a Universal consciousness or God exists, it is scientifically impossible for there not to be a creator. So scientifically we have examined God the Universal consciousness and found that the force is omnipotent, truly everywhere and all connected. And spiritually through sharing my own experience, we have seen the workings of a force bigger than us.

I hope this duality of discussion, both spiritual and scientific will help you the reader to see this first truth. God exists, and exists in a variety of forms, you will find God's work behind the Bible in parts, same goes for the

Quran, and the Vedas, the Hindu texts. You will find God all over this planet in a variety of forms and names and I hope together we have learned that God is not solely confined to one religion, but is in fact at work behind the scenes of all of them.

God is not confined to Islam nor Christianity, and if you believe that you only have the favour of God by being Christened, or by following the set doctrines of any other religion, or practising any other set doctrines of a set path, then sadly logic suggests you are wrong. I follow no road of religion, yet walk a path with God every day.

So, the first truth is that God exists, and is connected through the Universal consciousness. God is consciousness, manifesting and creating the material world. We are God's manifestation, God's ever evolving creation at work, and it is this closeness, this invisible bond that has compelled so many of our ancestors around the globe since the dawn of time to know something bigger is behind it all, and have thusly worshipped this supernatural force, giving our creator many different names over the time of man's existence.

The second truth, is the understanding of we, and the importance of we. I touched on this in the last chapter. Now we see together that the whole Universe is one connected energy, we should start to begin to reveal our similarities with others rather than our differences, as well as the connection to everything else in the Universe. We are truly one conscious entity.

Psychologically the majority of humanity is still in 'tribal' mode, as a people the world still sits in boxes of opposition from their fellow man. Even on this simple subject of a creator, God, we can look at the world and still find conflict within a field that should truly be free from any violence, or aggressive debate.

Once we as a people release our social, cultural, ethnic and religious beliefs we get left with what God truly created...Humans! Our greatest similarity, and our brotherhood of man and woman. Isn't this what we should be celebrating and embracing?

My relationship with God has been as soul satisfying from the beginning of my journey in life, right up to this point in my life sat here concluding my book, and I, like mentioned before never go to any 'formal' place of worship. The light, the love, and the understanding of all comes from within. Your inner journey of releasing ego and fear will help hugely in accepting others regarding their own particular culture and their views. Until you know and accept yourself, you will never know how to change for the better. Once you lovingly accept your own flaws you will find it so much easier to accept other people's.

If you're reading this believing you are perfect, then please pop that little bubble. We can all be better and do much more, each and every one of us, every day, in every way. We are spirits, beings of conscious energy living and learning manifested in a material human body. We make mistakes naturally, and everyday can be a challenge, but this is the meaning of life. We are reflecting in miniature scale, the life and evolution of our Universe. We are born and we grow and evolve physically, mentally and if consciously aware spiritually, into individual realities, each distinctly different from the next person's reality, and at the end we die, hopefully passing on our learned information to our children, so that their lives are a better version than the lives we had.

This is exactly what the Universe or nature is continuously doing. It self learns, evolves. Species die out, new species arrive. We just, as all living things do, continually send information back to our conscious source, God. This information exchange all happens within the quantum realm, a continuous connection with our source. With this information interchange the Universal consciousness grows and so does our own, both parties involved becoming a better version than their former self. This is the meaning of life, the expansion of God's consciousness, alongside our own in continuous evolution.

The Universal consciousness, God, just like we do contemplates its own spiritual conscious self, and learns from the manifestation of its own polar opposite form, matter, just as we do. Where the Universe is in fact the Universal consciousness creating the matter based realm we see around us. We in reality are the same consciousness as the Universe, living out our days in a material living shell. Separate yet all the time together. Just as when we die, the consciousness leaves the material shell. Just as when our Universe ends the Universal consciousness, God will do the same and a Universe will begin all over again. I touched on this before. Consciousness was there before the 'Big bang', and exists outside the realm of matter, space and time. Therefore, when the Universe ends so will time, space and matter. The consciousness however will keep on going. We mirror our Universe in life and death in so many ways. We all come from the same source. So, embrace the similarities of your fellow man and woman and accept their differences. Universally we are all one, and even on a material level of existence, it is scientifically proven through DNA that we have all descended from Mitochondrial Eve some 144,000 years ago. We truly are all brothers and sisters.

The first truth is God exists, the second truth is the

importance of, and the acceptance of we.

Quite obviously the first truth is important, without the acceptance of the grandeur and complexity of God's Universe, how can you possibly believe in the third truth. The third truth is of divine importance, not just for you but for the whole of humanity also.

The third truth I have discovered on my journey is the 'realisation of self' and the importance of 'self', utilising the law of 'cause and effect', the realisation of the power of self and its role in the Universe as a creator of what is. We have incredible power at our disposal in that we hold the key to a happy existence compared to a miserable one.

Just consider the popular used saying, 'do you see the glass as half empty or half full?' How can one equal measurement have two opposite outcomes and views based purely on perspective? Clearly it comes from the viewers' personal perspective on life.

We from within actually control which response we choose to have, whether it be a negative one or a positive one. And this small example can be used to reflect our entire existence. Just think at how different your life would be if you had approached every situation in life with a more positive outlook. We tend to get in life what we think we deserve in life. This alone is the key to happiness and fulfilment of self, it is soul enriching rather than soul destroying.

What is key to understand here is that thought is at the beginning of all creation. There is nothing in this world that we use from day to day, that hasn't had its initial stage of creation from a thought. Your thoughts are the very first stage of creation. Monitor your thoughts, your thoughts will manifest a positive or a negative reality. They will dictate whether you have good relationships with the ones close to you in life or an estranged one. And with keen development of the first truth and acceptance of being connected to a higher power slowly the Universal consciousness will be opened for you. And it is here where you find all the answers deep down that you already knew. Have you ever heard something or read something and then after a few moments thought that you have never heard it or thought it before and yet it rings so much truth to you within? Some will relate to this, others won't, but this is the Universal consciousness, eureka moments, indescribable with words.

Not only do we have the power of creation at our hands regarding how we perceive the world around us and hence affect our own reality, whether it is a positive existence or a negative one. But we also have the power through constant conscious aware thought, or being 'in the now' as discussed in earlier chapters, to manifest a better version of our self, with again thought being the first level involved, this time in the creation of ourselves. The implications of these two points regarding the third truth of the importance and realisation of 'the self' are huge. This simple truth lived everyday will change your entire life, and change the lives of those around you. It will not happen overnight, nothing great ever does, and if it was easy everyone would do it, so be patient.

Praying is an interesting concept. There is nothing wrong in praying as long as it is for the strength to take whatever challenge you need to take on. Praying for change will not bring change, but praying for the strength to change ourselves and our attitude towards this life in a positive way will bring change. I personally do not pray very often. I will sit in a quiet place and be thankful, and every once in a while, visualise that which I know I deserve, but I never ask in prayer. The Universal consciousness or God, sees the world through my eyes, why would I ask that which knows all about me and already know that which I seek? Isn't asking itself questioning the very presence of God? Be thankful in prayer for those things you know are coming, and dream big! Seeing what you want in your mind's eye is the first level of creation. Now that it has been created in mind, it is already on its way to you. Subconsciously these steps in prayer or thought will engage us onto the path of finding and realising our creation. We get in life what we believe we deserve in life, not what we want in life.

It is easy to exist on a lower level of reality, being ignorant to anyone else in the world, and only interacting with those that serve you. It is easy to live in this selfish way, a way that only serves you. If you choose this path you will be very lonely or if you do have friends, then they will simply be friends on a similar level. The old saying is true, 'birds of a feather, flock together', or the one I prefer, 'like attracts like'. This last saying helps us best understand one of the important consequences of changing for the better. The more aware and conscious you become, the more your thoughts will begin to change to more positive ones, positive thoughts yield positive action and naturally positive results.

Similarly, the higher the level of consciousness you choose to live on, the higher the expectations you will have for yourself. This positive change applied throughout your life will allow for more positive relationships, better work moral, a happier more fulfilling existence. Naturally you will attract people around you that also either live this way or envy your new outlook and also wish to live the way you do. All positive. 'Like attracts like', when you begin to become divine (as the Universe intended) in your actions and thoughts, and develop yourself both inwardly and outwardly you will start to become as great as you can be. Your yields will also be divine and as great as they can be. It is a simple case of 'cause and effect'.

Like touched on earlier in the chapter, we mirror God in essence within our own consciousness or spirit. Like the Universe was created and manifested by God so do we also manifest and create the world around us. We are all creators. Each and every one of us. This is the greatest gift we hold. The journey is hard but it is worth it. Everything you have right now in life is a result of your own actions. If it is bad change it, only you can create the reality you so desire. Like I said at the beginning of this book, what I say here has been said before, many times, but now we clearly have the support scientifically that our Universe is not just a vast space of inert material with the odd scattering of life amongst the stars that somehow arrived by a miracle. The Universe is alive, a conscious whole connected to you, embrace it, nurture it and love it. It used to sound like fantasy mumbo jumbo without the science. And now we discover that it is science fact and not science fiction.

So then, summing it up is simple. The first truth is that the Universal consciousness, God exists. The second truth is to accept your fellow human, even if you do not fully understand them. And the final truth, be the creator you were born to be and become the change you seek in your world. When you begin to develop a more positive, 'self-awareness' you will begin to see more positivity in the world. Monitor your thoughts all the time, as we are in life what we think about in life. This world, this reality, is only what you think of it. Journey inwards and learn to know yourself. Journey outwards and learn about the world around you. Learn from experience and not simply from someone's own personal opinion. Learn to believe that you deserve more, because it is true, we get in life what we believe we deserve in life. Be the person God designed you to be, as no one else will ever be you better than you. And finally discover and embrace your purpose, eventually millions of years from now all this will be gone and forgotten, life is short, transient, so be the best you can be, you are only here once and the world needs you to be you more than ever. You are a key in the workings of an evolution of Universal consciousness that spans the existence of everything, even time itself. You should realise now that your life and your existence is important and is imperative in the evolution of our Universe and God itself.

    More than anything else I hope you begin to question. Question everything just like a child does, in questioning you will reveal so much that will contradict what you thought you knew. Enjoy life, every way and every day. You are here now and life is ever so short, so enjoy it and embrace it. One day you will die and your own unique Universe will die with you, accept this wholeheartedly. Accepting death is important in appreciating life. Do not wait for life to teach you this sobering lesson.

    And finally, thank you. Thank you for taking the time to read what I have shared within the pages of this book. I truly hope that this book either confirms what you already thought or at least opens your mind up to questioning rather than just accepting the things that you are taught, shown or told in this life.

The beginning.

End Notes

Introduction

1
https://www.scientificamerican.com/article/something-from-nothing-vacuum-can-yield-flashes-of-light/

The Mind Trap.

2   Henry David Thoreau

3. Winston Churchill.

4 . Hippocrates.

Releasing Ego And Fear and Discovering Our True Self
5. Mahatma Ghandi

The Pine Cone.
Figure 1.
http://www.mindserpent.com/American_History/religion/pope/bg/osiris_pine_cone_staff.jpg

Figure 2.
https://commons.wikimedia.org/wiki/File:Cortile_della_Pigna_pine_cone_2.jpg   (public domain file 1/1/2017) *This Wikipedia and Wikimedia Commons image is from the user Wknight94 and is freely available under the creative commons cc-by-sa 3.0 license.*

Figure 3.
https://en.wikipedia.org/wiki/Marduk#/media/File:Apada

na_winged_man.jpg (public domain file 1/1/2017)

Figure 4.
https://commons.wikimedia.org/wiki/File:Lord_Shiva_Images_-_An_artistic_representation_of_Lord_Shiva_and_the_12_Jyotirlingas_associated_with_him.jpg (public domain file 1/1/17)

Figure 5.
https://commons.wikimedia.org/wiki/File:BuddhaStThailand.jpg
(Public domain file 1/1/17)

The Mark Of The Creator. Intelligent Design.
Figure 6.
https://commons.wikimedia.org/wiki/File:Golden_ratio_line.svg
(Public domain file 3/1/17)

Figure 7.
https://upload.wikimedia.org/wikipedia/commons/0/08/NautilusCutawayLogarithmicSpiral.jpg

This Wikipedia and Wikimedia Commons image is from the user Chris 73 and is freely available at //commons.wikimedia.org/wiki/File:NautilusCutawayLogarithmicSpiral.jpg under the creative commons cc-by-sa 3.0 license Figure 8.
https://commons.wikimedia.org/wiki/File:Fibonacci_spiral_34.svg
(Public domain file 1/1/17)

Figure 9.
https://commons.wikimedia.org/wiki/File:Aeonium_tabul

iforme.jpg
(public file from wikimedia user Max Ronnersjö under license 3.0)

Figure 10.
https://commons.wikimedia.org/wiki/File:Bromelia.png
(public domain file 1/1/17)

Figure 11.
https://commons.wikimedia.org/wiki/File:Joconde.gif
(Free file from wikipedia under license 2.5. Original upload from user Castorpuntoes

Figure 12.
https://commons.wikimedia.org/wiki/File:Atom_diagram.png
(Permission granted from user Fastfission on wikipedia, under the Free documentation license version 1.2 and license and the attribution-share alike 3.0 unported license)

Figure 13.
https://upload.wikimedia.org/wikipedia/commons/c/c2/Solar_sys.jpg
(Public domain file 2/1/17. NASA file.)

6. *Earnest Rutherford.*
Everything Is Connected And Everything Is One.
7. http://www.users.csbsju.edu/~frioux/quantumqts.html

8. http://newrepublic.com/article/116187/scientists-can-levitate-objects-using-sound-waves

The 33, 333 Phenomenon.

Figure 14.
https://en.wikipedia.org/wiki/File:Om_symbol.svg
 (Public domain file 1/1/17)

Figure 15.
https://commons.wikimedia.org/wiki/File:Allah3.svg
 (Public Domain File 1/1/17)

Figure 16.
https://commons.wikimedia.org/wiki/File:Clock-in-cairo-with-eastern-arabic-numerals.jpg (public domain file 1/1/17)

Figure 17.
https://commons.wikimedia.org/wiki/File:Lord_Shiva_Images_-_An_artistic_representation_of_Lord_Shiva_and_the_12_Jyotirlingas_associated_with_him.jpg (public domain file 1/1/17)

Figure 18.
https://commons.wikimedia.org/wiki/File:Cambodian_-_The_Hindu_God_Brahma_-_Walters_542734.jpg
(File free to use under the Crerative commons attribution-share alike 3.0 unported license from user Walters Art Museum.)

Figure 19.
https://commons.wikimedia.org/wiki/File:Star_of_David.svg
(Public domain file copyright free. 1/1/17)

Figure 20.
https://commons.wikimedia.org/wiki/File:Sikh_symbol.jpg

(Copyright free public domain image. 1/1/2017)

Printed in Germany
by Amazon Distribution
GmbH, Leipzig